NO FOREIGN OIL ON U.S. SOIL

TURNING WASTED ENERGY INTO WEALTH WITH HYDROGEN POWER FOR AMERICA

RICK SEYMOUR

Published by

BEVERLY HILLS PUBLISHING™

468 N. Camden Drive

Beverly Hills, CA 90210

Beverly Hills Publishing™

www.beverlyhillspublishing.com

ISBN: 979-8-9991490-7-7

To my **nephew Chris,**

I know it was you who, in some unseen way, made this book deal happen. My only wish is that you could be here to enjoy this journey with me. I carry your spirit with me on every page.
To my **mother**, **Leora,** who always loved, cared for, and understood me. Who let me be exactly who I was. To my **father, Alan,** who pushed me to dream big, make something of myself, and who reminded me every day that I could do better—that I *must* do better. His voice still drives me.

To my **family**. **Shelly**, **Rachel**, and **John**,

What began as a lighthearted Friday night joke somehow became a global idea. Your support, patience, laughter, and love turned that moment into a movement. Rachel, thank you for being the one to say, *"You can write this book."* That was all I needed.

And above all, to **God**,

For saving my life more times than I can count. For giving me the vision to see what others could not. And, for trusting me to carry an idea that can help transform the United States, and hopefully, in some small way, the world.

Thank you.

Contents

Acknowledgements

This book is the result of lifetime curiosity, persistence, and support from those who believed in me, often before I believed in myself.

I begin by expressing my deep appreciation to the **Boy Scouts of America**, whose values profoundly shaped my early years. From them, I learned the importance of avoiding waste, being a good steward of the environment, and acting as a responsible citizen—not just for my country, but for the world. These guiding principles became the moral foundation of this book, offering power and utility companies a practical, profitable path forward. One that aligns business success with national service.

To my **eighth-grade chemistry teacher, Mr Patton**. Thank you for introducing me to the process of making hydrogen. That single experiment lit a fire that has burned for over 50 years.

To my **college chemistry professor.** I will never forget the moment you ignited a hydrogen balloon in our auditorium and said, *"Whoever figures out how to make hydrogen cheaply will be an overnight millionaire."* That vision became my driving force—my version of the golden goose.

I am grateful to my **brother-in-law, Ricky Hintgen,** for his patience in answering my many questions early on. I am thankful to my **brother, Ron Seymour**, for being the one I could always count on to help with electrical and technical details, bringing my ideas to life.

To my business partner and mentor, **Tim Razzari**. Your insight still rings in my ears. When I presented the concept for a clean car race, you said, *"If everything you're saying is true, how are you going to make money on it?"* That question kept me focused on the realities of execution and profitability lessons that shaped the pages ahead.

To my long-term friend, **Leonard Redwine**. Thank you for your unwavering support. For more than 35 years, you clipped and sent me every hydrogen-related article you could find. You believed in my vision when others laughed. I will never forget that.

Finally, to my **family**. To my loving wife **Shelly**, my son **John**, and my daughter **Rachel,** thank you from the bottom of my heart. Your love, patience, and encouragement carried me through the long hours, setbacks, and late-night brainstorming sessions. I know I can be stubborn, and I know this journey has not always been easy. But your support has meant everything to me. This book is as much yours as it is mine.

Introduction:

Jules Verne

"I believe that water will one day be employed as fuel, that hydrogen and oxygen, which constitute it, used singly or together, will furnish an inexhaustible source of heat and light, of an intensity of which coal is not capable."

— From "The Mysterious Island" (1874)

A Personal Discovery

I first learned about hydrogen in eighth-grade science class. We split water into hydrogen and oxygen through electrolysis, taking water and turning it into fuel. It seemed like magic. What I didn't realize then was that this magic would become my life's mission.

Years later, I began working in car sales and spent over 40 years in manufacturing, the automotive industry, and running successful businesses, and I saw how our inefficient energy use was destroying value on a massive scale. Wars, climate change, the push for green energy, and a shifting global economy all made one thing clear: America's energy dependence is neither sustainable nor wise.

The Energy Crisis We're Ignoring

For over three decades, I've watched our nation send trillions of dollars overseas for oil, while at home, we throw away enough energy to power our country. According to the U.S. Energy Information Administration (EIA), in 2023, some of the top five countries exporting oil to the United States were not our staunch allies.[1] Meanwhile, we're wasting over two-thirds of the energy we produce right here. This does not make sense—economically, politically, or morally.

A Simple, Practical Solution

Here's the good news: we already have everything we need to fix this. We don't need to invent new technology or undertake decades-long infrastructure projects. The solution is ready to be implemented. By capturing "wasted" electricity—power that utilities often pay others to take off their hands or end up curtailing (shutting off)—we can use existing American manufacturing capabilities and the most abundant resource on Earth to generate clean hydrogen fuel: water.

Why Start with Medium and Heavy-Duty Trucks?

When we talk about transitioning to hydrogen, medium and heavy-duty trucks are a great starting point. They currently account for a substantial percentage of emissions—up to 28%.[2] The technology to convert these vehicles to hydrogen power isn't some far-off dream: Kenworth/Toyota, Hyzon, and other manufacturers are already building hydrogen-powered trucks.[3] By connecting the dots between our wasted energy and these trucks, we can jump-start an energy revolution in the United States.

Who This Book Is For:

- **Utility Companies**: Learn how to turn curtailed energy and negative pricing problems into a new profit center.
- **American Manufacturers**: Discover how to expand into producing fuel cell trucks and electrolyzers for hydrogen fuel, including Hydrogen storage tanks
- **Fleet Managers**: Slash fuel costs while helping our country move toward true energy independence.
- **Investors**: Realize this moment is a pivotal opportunity comparable to the early days of oil.

Why Now?

Every day we continue to depend on foreign oil, we remain vulnerable to external influences and geopolitical pressures. Every day we waste energy that could power millions of homes is a day we lag in the race for clean, stable, and affordable energy. The solution isn't theoretical.

I've studied every angle: chemistry, economics, and policy. I have talked with utility companies, manufacturers, and government officials. I've learned plenty of ways hydrogen projects can fail, but I've also seen exactly why they can succeed.

What You'll Learn

1. **Why Batteries Alone Aren't Enough**: Storing energy solely within batteries is limited and does not address all our grid and transportation needs.
2. **How Hydrogen Stabilizes the Grid**: Using hydrogen production to absorb excess electricity solves curtailment issues while creating fuel for heavy transportation.
3. **A 12-Month Implementation Plan**: Step-by-step strategies for rolling out hydrogen infrastructure and vehicle conversion quickly, without waiting decades.
4. **Nationwide Benefits**: Whether you're farming in Iowa or running a tech startup in California, hydrogen power can reduce costs, bolster energy independence, and strengthen local economies.

A Call to Action

It's tempting to say we need more studies or "proof of concept" projects, but time is not on our side. If there's one thing I've learned, it's that the best solutions are often the simplest; they just require the courage to act. Henry Ford revolutionized transportation by simplifying it. We can similarly revolutionize American energy.

We stand at a crossroads: continue down the path of foreign oil dependence and wasting the resources we have, or choose a future of energy dominance, environmental sustainability, and national prosperity. This book is your roadmap—written in plain English so everyone, from CEOs to policy-makers to concerned citizens, can join the hydrogen revolution.

Let's stop throwing away our energy. Let's stop sending our wealth overseas. Let's work together to build an energy-independent America that benefits us all.

Welcome to the hydrogen revolution. Let's get started!

Chapter 1:

Understanding the Financial Benefits of Hydrogen

To fully understand the financial benefits explored in this book, it is essential to grasp a few foundational concepts in electricity, hydrogen production, and energy economics. At the heart of this opportunity is the process of converting wasted electricity into hydrogen through electrolysis. This chapter lays the groundwork for that understanding.

Basic Electricity: Watts, Kilowatts, Megawatts, and Gigawatts

A **watt (W)** is the basic unit of power in electricity, measuring the rate at which energy is being used or generated.

- 1,000 watts = 1 **kilowatt (kW)**
- 1,000 kilowatts = 1 **megawatt (MW)**
- 1,000 megawatts = 1 **gigawatt (GW)**

Power usage over time is measured in **kilowatt-hours (kWh)**, **megawatt-hours (MWh)**, or **gigawatt-hours (GWh)**.

Examples:

- 10 LED bulbs = 100 watts = 0.1 kW
- Microwave = 1 kW
- Small home A/C = 2 kW
- EV fast charger = 50–350 kW
- Wind turbine = 2,000–3,000 kW (2–3 MW)
- Large utility-scale solar plant = 100 MW
- Major power station or regional grid = 1 GW or more

Household usage:

- Average U.S. home = ~30 kWh/day, or 900 kWh/month

Electricity is sold in **kWh**, which is how your energy bill is calculated.

What Is Gasoline Gallon Equivalent (GGE)?

Fuel Type	Energy Content	GGE Equivalent
Gasoline	114,000 BTU/gallon	1.00 GGE
Diesel	128,700 BTU/gallon	1.13 GGE
Hydrogen	33.3 kWh/kg (~120,000 BTU)	1.00 GGE

GGE is used to compare fuels based on energy content: **Takeaway:**

- 1 kg of hydrogen = ~1 GGE
- 1 gallon of diesel = ~1.13 GGE
- Hydrogen fuel-cell vehicles can get **50–70 miles/kg**. This is often better than gasoline or diesel per GGE.

Electrolysis: Turning Water into Hydrogen

Electrolysis splits water into hydrogen (H2) and oxygen (O2) using electricity:

1. Water goes into an **electrolyzer**
2. Electricity splits water molecules
3. Hydrogen is captured and stored as clean fuel

Electricity Requirements:

- It takes **50–55 kWh** to produce **1 kg of hydrogen**
- Electrolyzer efficiency: 60%–70%

System Output Example:

- 1 MW electrolyzer → 20 kg of H2/hour = 480 kg/day
- At $5/kg retail → $2,400/day in hydrogen revenue

Water Requirements for Hydrogen Production

Hydrogen production consumes purified water:

- **1 kg of hydrogen = 9 liters (2.4 gallons) of water**
- Compared to:

Hydrogen Output	Water Needed
1 kg	9 liters (2.4 gal)
10 kg	90 liters (23.8 gal)
1 ton (1,000 kg)	9,000 liters (2,378 gal)

- Gasoline refining uses 3–6 gallons of water per gallon of fuel
- Producing one cotton t-shirt: 2,700 liters of water

Hydrogen with **recycled wastewater** becomes even more sustainable.

Energy Curtailment: The Hidden Source of Wealth

Curtailment is when energy that could be produced is **wasted** because:

1. **Oversupply** – too much renewable power, not enough demand
2. **Transmission limits** – power can't reach its destination
3. **Grid congestion** – local lines overloaded with solar/wind power
4. **Market economics** – negative electricity prices
5. **No storage** – no batteries or hydrogen to store the excess

U.S. Examples:

- California curtailed over **2.5 million MWh** in 2023
- Wind curtailment is rising in Texas and the Midwest

Opportunity:

Wasted electricity can be captured and fed into electrolyzers to make **hydrogen**.

This will:

- Stabilize the grid
- Prevent waste
- Create valuable fuel
- Enable local energy resilience

Conclusion: From Wasted Energy to National Wealth

Understanding the basics of electricity, fuel equivalency, electrolysis, water usage, and curtailment is the key to unlocking hydrogen's economic promise. What was once thrown away can now become a cornerstone of clean transportation, energy storage, and industrial fuel. This book shows how we turn that potential into profit.

Chapter 2:

The Hidden Costs of Foreign Oil Dependence

It was 1973, and I was thirteen years old. For hours, my father and I sat in a line snaking around the block, waiting for gas. His knuckles turned white on the steering wheel, and our car's engine was turned off. Overnight, the price of gas had jumped from 25 cents to nearly two dollars a gallon.[4] But this wasn't just about money—it was about helplessness. How could the most powerful nation on Earth be brought to its knees by countries halfway around the world?

Fifty years later, America is still addicted to foreign oil—we've just gotten better at hiding the cost. Thousands of oil tankers crisscross our oceans daily, burning diesel fuel and leaving oil slicks in their wake. We shrug and call it "the cost of doing business." But consider this: every three days, we send about a billion dollars overseas for oil. That's over 150 billion dollars a year—money that could be repairing crumbling roads or funding our schools. Instead, it bolsters nations that don't exactly cheer for America's success.[5]

The monetary price is just the start. I've watched families send their sons and daughters to fight in distant deserts, the Gulf War in Kuwait, and conflicts that "aren't about oil" yet always seem to revolve around it.[6] We're told it's for freedom or democracy. But if those places didn't have oil, would our troops be stationed there at all?

Hidden costs go deeper still. Every time we fill up our tanks, we're not just paying at the pump—we are also paying for a massive military presence to protect shipping lanes, for cleanup after catastrophic spills, and for the healthcare costs of pollution.[7] Ultimately, we remain vulnerable to any foreign power that decides to squeeze our energy supply. Every crisis in the Middle East eventually finds its way to the American wallet.

But here's the most frustrating part: we don't have to live like this. In the U.S., we are throwing away enough energy to power our entire transportation system. While we spend billions importing foreign oil, utility companies pay producers to shut down solar and wind farms because our energy grid can't handle the excess. It's like standing in a grocery store, tossing two-thirds of the food into the trash, then placing an order for expensive takeout from halfway across the world.

In this chapter, we'll delve into what foreign oil dependence really costs us—not just in dollars, but in blood, security, and missed opportunities too. More importantly, you'll see why we're at a turning point. For the first time in history, we have everything we need to break free from this dependency. And first, we need to understand exactly what we're paying for in our current system. It might make you angry—it should—but that anger can drive the change we desperately need.

Beyond the Pump: The True Price We Pay

Consider my friend who runs an automotive company. In 2008, he was at lunch with me and a local real estate builder who held around one million dollars in a local bank stock. The builder asked me what I thought of the housing market. I told him I had a bad feeling—a major bank like Washington Mutual might fail. I also told him that I heard rumors that his local bank, County Bank of Merced, might be in trouble. He laughed, saying his bank was rock solid. That was Wednesday.

"By Friday of that same week, Bear Stearns' shares plunged from $160 to $2.[8] Within three months, Washington Mutual was gone, and that "rock solid" local bank's stock fell from $22 to $0.78. The builder lost every penny.[9]

Why bring this up in a discussion about oil dependence? Because it shows how hidden vulnerabilities can explode without warning. Our reliance on foreign oil works the same way: it's a systemic risk nobody sees until it's too late.

Let's break down the real cost at the pump. Sure, there's the per-gallon price, but that's just the tip of the iceberg. From exploration teams that burn fossil fuels to find more oil, to the drilling rigs drilling for oil, to trucks or pipelines pumping the crude oil onto tankers. Then the tankers cross the oceans, unload at the refineries, and finally, the trucks that deliver it to our local gas stations. Each step relies on and consumes massive amounts of fossil fuels.

It's like paying interest on an interest-only loan: our economy is built on a resource we barely control. Protecting shipping lanes requires a massive U.S. military presence around the world—another hidden tax every American pays, driver or not. And when the inevitable spill, accident, or political conflict hits, costs shoot up exponentially. Remember the gas lines of the 1970s? Those lines did more than test our patience, they triggered a recession that shattered American families and small businesses.

In short, we have built our economic house on land someone else owns. Eventually, the owner will show up with a bill we can't ignore. The good news? It doesn't have to be this way.

Trade Imbalances: How We're Mortgaging America's Future

Here's why we don't have to live like this: right now, America wastes enough clean energy to power our entire transportation system.[10] In 2023, we imported around 6.48 million barrels of crude oil a day at roughly $70 a barrel—that is $453 million (using an average of 6 million barrels imported at $70 per barrel, the average is $420 million), leaving the country daily.[11] Every three days, we're sending more than a billion dollars overseas. That money could be staying in our communities, improving our infrastructure, and creating American jobs.

I've seen both sides of this equation. I grew up in the Midwest, watching farmers lease land for wind turbines, only to have their energy production curtailed because the grid can't handle it. Then, in California, solar farms have to shut down their solar arrays on sunny days because there's nowhere to store all the extra energy. While we discard this renewable power, we continue to write billion-dollar checks to foreign oil producers.

If you think that's absurd, consider this: we also export around 10.15 million barrels of oil a day. We do it by refining foreign crude oil and shipping out the finished products, including gasoline and diesel.[12] It's the equivalent of running a restaurant *and* borrowing ingredients from your competitors. Yes, it keeps the doors open in the short term, but it also keeps us hostage to external forces beyond our control.

The biggest irony of all? There's no need for any of it. We can use all of our wasted power—not just solar and wind—to power America. Excess wind in Iowa could run most of the trucking industry in that state. Excess solar in California could charge fleets of electric and hydrogen vehicles. **The three largest California power companies are in the gas business, yet they don't see the opportunity right in front of them**. Still, we maintain the old status quo, funneling billions overseas and letting domestic resources go to waste.

Breaking Free: America's Path to Energy Independence

Every morning, I still wake up anxious about world events that could send oil prices skyrocketing: unrest (which drastically affects the stock market) in the Middle East, a decision by OPEC, or a blocked tanker route. This lingering fear is a habit formed over decades in business—one our children shouldn't have to inherit.

The hidden costs of foreign oil dependence—massive military bills, environmental damage, economic vulnerability—are not laws of nature. They are products of our choices, and choices can be reversed. In 1973, we had no ready alternative. Today, we do. We are paying utility companies to shut down wind and solar farms and other power plants throughout the day instead of harnessing that power for our cars and heavy-duty trucks, businesses, and homes. "That's the way we've always done it," simply isn't a valid excuse anymore.

In the coming chapters, you'll discover how America's greatest untapped resource—our wasted energy—can be transformed into fuel. You'll learn why hydrogen technology isn't just a hopeful trend; it is a real, viable key to energy independence. Companies like Toyota are already building trucks and cars that run on hydrogen, and other automakers are following suit.[13] Our utilities are poised to become the energy providers of tomorrow, turning curtailed power into an incredible opportunity using energy that otherwise would have been **WASTED**.

Most crucially, this isn't some pie-in-the-sky plan that will take decades. We have the infrastructure to start making these changes tomorrow, using technology that already exists. The hidden costs of oil dependence weigh heavily on us, but we can shut them down. We have everything we need to break free—we just need to decide to do it.

What will happen once oil stops being the #1 source for transportation fuel in the United States? Will our economy become stronger and economically friendly to all Americans through the use of clean and renewable hydrogen fuel?

Conclusion for Chapter 2

America's addiction to foreign oil has shaped our lives for decades, often in ways we barely notice until a crisis arrives. In this chapter, we discussed how the 1973 gas lines, military entanglements, and soaring costs at the pump are all facets of a broken system. We also looked at the enormous amounts of clean energy we waste each day—enough to power our entire transportation sector—while sending billions of dollars overseas for oil. It's a classic case of maintaining the status quo instead of embracing game-changing innovations.

Yet, there's a clear path forward. By harnessing curtailed wind, solar, and all other types of curtailed electricity, and adopting clean and renewable hydrogen as an alternative fuel. The transition to a clean, renewable energy source is easy to convert, **as well as highly profitable**. By transforming the role of our utility companies, we can finally liberate ourselves from the grip of foreign oil. This isn't a future dream, it's a present opportunity. The next chapters will show exactly how we can seize it, one step at a time.

Chapter 3:

America's Greatest Untapped Resource—Wasted Energy

At this very moment, an extraordinary paradox is unfolding across America: energy companies work tirelessly to meet our nation's growing power demands, yet billions of dollars' worth of electricity quietly vanishes into thin air. It's akin to a farmer harvesting a bumper crop of corn, only to burn two-thirds of it in the field for lack of proper storage.

We're wasting up to 66% of our generated power, not because we don't need it, but because we haven't built the infrastructure to harness it.[14] In the previous chapter, we saw how our foreign oil dependence drains our national security and economic stability. Now, we confront another hidden cost: the massive waste of domestic energy production—a resource that could be our ticket to true energy dominance.

To put this into perspective, in 2024, California curtailed over 3.4 million megawatt-hours of renewable energy.[15] Picture streams of gold flowing straight down the drain, and at the same time, we simultaneously import resources from overseas. The irony is that this wasted energy represents much more than lost power; it's a lost opportunity to break our dependence on foreign oil once and for all.

Consider the Southwest's peak solar production hours. Often, as sunshine floods desert solar farms, they shut down production because the grid can't handle the surplus.[16] Yet, several hours later, fossil fuel plants fire up to meet evening demand. It's like watching fresh water run off into the ocean while parched communities scramble to drill deeper wells.

The challenge we face isn't generation—we're already producing more than enough energy. The real challenge is energy capture and storage, what I call ECS: Energy Capture with Hydrogen Storage. Traditional battery solutions can hold power for a matter of hours. But what if we could store surplus electricity for days, weeks, or even months? *What if this "waste" could be converted into a form that powers trucks, heats homes, and drives entire industries, including steel and cement?*

This chapter explores America's greatest untapped resource: the power we generate and fail to harness. We will dive into why this happens, what it costs, and how we can transform this liability into an asset. From utilities paying others to take their excess power, to innovative hydrogen conversion technologies that can store surplus energy indefinitely, the path to energy independence and better use of the energy we already produce may lie less in increased production and more in making the grid energy efficient and profitable.

The Power We're Paying to Throw Away: America's Multi-Billion Dollar Energy Paradox

Imagine running a restaurant that must prepare three times more meals than it can sell, only to pay someone to haul away the wasted food. This scenario mirrors what America's utility companies face daily, except instead of food, they're dealing with massive amounts of electric power.

In 2023, Texas curtailed 60 gigawatts of renewable energy—enough power to produce 1.2 billion kilograms of hydrogen fuel; this is roughly $5 billion lost that could have been captured and sold. This economic absurdity becomes even clearer when we look at ***negative pricing:*** utilities pay other entities to take power off their hands during surplus.[17]

The Great Plains provide another example: Southwest Power Pool (SPP). Wind turbines spin throughout the night, generating power that often can't be used. SPP has wasted 800 megawatt-hours every day for a year.[18] That's enough electricity to produce 16,000 kilograms of hydrogen every hour, every day, all year long. Do you think that the windmill investors could use an extra, say, 1,500,000 dollars a day? Would that be able to reduce the cost of our electric bill? The environmental toll of this squandered energy is immense, but so is the missed economic opportunity. Each curbed megawatt-hour could produce about 20 kilograms of hydrogen; at 5 dollars per kilogram retail price, it is like watching 100 dollar bills blow away in the wind.

Grid operators understand this problem intimately. Sophisticated control centers, resembling NASA mission control, monitor real-time power flows. Yet these operators frequently shut down production, not because the energy isn't needed, but because we lack the infrastructure to store and transport it. If we were to capture and convert this wasted energy into hydrogen, the payoffs would be transformative: utility companies' fleets (like PG&E) would become self-sustaining, and municipalities could swap expensive diesel trucks for zero-emission hydrogen-powered vehicles. The power is already being generated; we just need a better way to use it.

Understanding Grid Curtailment: The Great American Energy Spillway

America's electrical grid is like a vast system of rivers and dams, power flowing along transmission lines that crisscross the country. In giant control rooms, operators orchestrate these flows to prevent flooding or overloading, while ensuring communities receive enough power. Unlike water, though, electricity can't simply be collected in a reservoir when there's too much. When a surge of power arrives—midday from solar farms in the desert or wind farms in the middle of a gusty night—grid operators must decide which sources to curtail to avoid overwhelming the grid.

California Independent System Operators (CAISO), for instance, watches real-time data on massive displays. When congestion—think traffic jams for electrons—reaches critical levels, operators shut down solar fields first, then wind farms. Ironically, these same areas often need more power a few hours later. In 2023, California wasted enough renewable energy to power millions of homes, simply because it couldn't store or transport the surplus to where it was most needed.[19]

This curtailment trend has grown dramatically in recent years. Each event represents a tragic loss of potential. Every time clean energy is dumped, fossil fuel plants typically ramp up later, compounding cost and pollution. It is inefficient, expensive, and detrimental to the environment.

But the real crisis isn't whether we have enough energy, it's that we keep spilling excess energy when we could be storing it. Hydrogen production offers a solution akin to building a large reservoir; instead of letting energy spill over the dam, we can convert it into a flexible, storable fuel. The best part of hydrogen storage is that it can be stored underground in abandoned salt caverns.

Case Study: California's 60 Million Kilogram Opportunity: The Golden State's Green Energy Goldmine

In California's renewable energy landscape lies an extraordinary chance to reshape the state's entire transportation sector. For those driving down Interstate 5, rows of solar panels may just look like part of the scenery. In reality, these panels represent an untapped energy source capable of fueling fleets of trucks—an "oil field" in plain sight.

In 2023, California curtailed over 3 million megawatt-hours of renewable energy, enough to produce around 60 million kilograms of green hydrogen. At current diesel prices—around $5 per gallon—this could translate to $300 million in unrealized fuel value every year.

Utilities like Pacific Gas & Electric (PG&E) exemplify this missed opportunity. With a fleet of 14,000 medium and heavy-duty vehicles, PG&E spends millions annually on diesel, even as it pays others to take excess power off its hands. Every megawatt-hour of curtailed electricity could make about 20 kilograms of hydrogen—enough to power a semi-truck for 240 to 300 miles; this is enough hydrogen to power all service trucks for PG&E, Southern California Edison, and the Los Angeles Department of Water and Power (LADWP). This means California's current curtailment could fuel all three major utility companies' fleet of trucks with zero-emissions without building another solar panel or wind turbine.

Large industrial players, like Foster Farms in the Central Valley of California, could also capture and use surplus energy and convert it into hydrogen onsite, fueling their trucks, forklifts, and heating water for steam to clean the processing plant. They would also be capable of generating electricity during peak demand. The double benefit is that California could slash its carbon footprint while reducing foreign oil dependence. All it takes is for power producers, like PG&E, to install an electrolyzer on their company property and have Ford build the hydrogen-powered trucks, making this an easy solution to turn wasted energy into a storable, high-value fuel. How much cheaper would our electric bill be if PG&E didn't pay Arizona utility companies to buy their power?

From Liability to Asset: How America's Greatest Energy Waste Could Become Its Greatest Strength

America's energy landscape doesn't need a miracle breakthrough; it simply needs us to rethink our approach to how we store energy and expand the markets, so that we can capitalize on it. As we've learned, the amount of energy we currently curtail is enough to power large portions of our transportation sector and industries. Converting that waste into hydrogen makes sense economically and strategically.

When we add up the total curtailed energy across U.S. utilities, we're looking at a vast reservoir of power that could be used to produce billions of kilograms of hydrogen annually. Instead of spending millions to discard it—and billions more on foreign oil—we could invest in capturing this wasted energy resource here at home.

Every megawatt-hour of curtailed electricity represents unrealized potential. If converted to hydrogen, it could:

- Power heavy-duty trucks
- Heat industrial furnaces for steel and cement production
- Generate clean electricity during peak demand
- Provide storage capacity that surpasses any battery on the market
- Create millions of American jobs in manufacturing and clean energy production
- Pave the road to energy independence and dominance

The key isn't building more power plants but using what we have more intelligently. Hydrogen conversion can transform waste into profit, turning a liability that costs utilities millions into an asset worth billions. This approach demands a shift in how we think about storage: excess power and electricity are not a burden, but a gift waiting to be harnessed.

As we move forward, we'll see why traditional energy storage, particularly batteries, can't tackle this challenge alone; they have their place, but they lack the long-term capacity, safety, and scalability to solve our ever-growing surplus dilemma. Hydrogen, on the other hand, could capture and preserve these vast amounts of energy for days, weeks, or even months, bridging the gap between our abundant resources and unending energy needs.

Myth #1: Hydrogen is too expensive to use as a fuel!

If you are throwing away over 60% of all energy generated by the grid, if the electricity that you need is basically free, or in some cases, power companies pay people to take that electricity, then the myth that hydrogen is too expensive because of the cost of electricity simply is not true. Plus, when we expand biogas and biomass, the price of electricity will become less and less important.

Conclusion for Chapter 3

In Chapter 3, we uncovered the staggering scale of wasted energy across America and saw how curtailment throws away billions of dollars in potential power. We also learned that this isn't just an economic or environmental issue; it's a strategic opportunity to achieve genuine energy dominance. By converting surplus electricity into hydrogen, we can eliminate waste, reduce foreign oil reliance, and turn a liability into a national asset. The stage is set to explore why conventional battery storage can't solve this massive surplus challenge, and why hydrogen may be the key to unlocking America's untapped energy wealth.

Chapter 4:

The Eight-Hour Problem: Why Batteries Aren't Enough

I once stood at Castle Air Force Base watching B-52 bombers practice touch-and-go landings. Each massive plane carried enough fuel to power a small city for days, yet once airborne, they couldn't just plug into an outlet to keep flying. They needed portable, potent energy.

Our electrical grid faces a similar predicament. As we saw in the previous chapter, we generate enormous amounts of excess energy, only to waste it. Storing it in batteries might seem like an obvious fix, but here's the catch: most utility-scale batteries can only store about eight hours of power. After that, they're spent—just like a B-52 forced to land after an eight-hour flight (of course, without in-flight refueling).

This mismatch between energy production and storage capacity is what I call the Eight-Hour Problem. Even large-scale installations, like Moss Landing in California, the nation's biggest battery sites, can store only 4-8 hours' worth of electricity before hitting capacity. To capture all the excess energy we produce, we would need a battery the size of Nebraska—an idea that is neither practical nor cost-effective, especially given finite lithium resources.

The Limitations of Current Energy Storage: Why Scale Matters More Than Efficiency

Driving past the Moss Landing battery facility, you can't help but marvel at rows of high-tech battery units. It's impressive on the surface. There is enough power to supply around 250,000 homes for about four hours. Yet, once you do the math, you see how limited this solution is: storing one day's worth of California's curtailed renewable energy would require far more lithium than the world currently mines in a year.

Additionally, grid-scale battery storage is not as efficient as advertised, due to repeated AC-to-DC and DC-to-AC conversions—each step loses energy as heat. Facilities like Moss Landing, which recently experienced a huge fire and shutdowns, demonstrate the risk of pushing battery technology to (and beyond) its safe limits.[20]

Short-term, high-efficiency storage is where batteries thrive, being used in electric vehicles and consumer electronics. However, they help very little to back up power for data centers. And, using them to hold the vast seasonal surpluses of wind and solar energy is like trying to fill a swimming pool with a handful of drinking glasses. Even if you keep pouring, you won't solve the fundamental problem of scale.

The Problem with Unplanned Energy Transitions: Lessons from the Grid's Growing Pains

Moss Landing, built on the site of a retired natural gas plant, symbolizes the hasty shift toward batteries without a deeper plan. Grid operators see exactly where there's surplus power and where there's demand. Yet they often can't move energy efficiently or store it in sufficient quantities. The duck curve in California—where solar peaks at noon and demand peaks at dusk—illustrates this daily struggle.[21]

Advocates often focus on how "efficient" batteries can be at short-term energy delivery. But a Ferrari is also efficient at turning fuel into speed; that doesn't mean it's the right vehicle to transport wheat across the ocean. Batteries simply can't address large-scale, long-duration, heavy loads (like semi-trucks and heavy equipment). Nor do they have the ability to produce steel and cement. Hydrogen, on the other hand, does, making it the greater fuel source. Remember, batteries do not make electricity; they only store it.

For instance, at 2 AM in Iowa, during surplus wind production, a battery installation could quickly max out, and any further wind energy would be wasted. When we rely heavily on short-duration storage, we're paying to build partial solutions that can't handle a week of high winds or a season of variable solar output.

Learning from Past Infrastructure Mistakes: The High Cost of Rushed Solutions

In the 1990s, during my time in autosales, I watched families buy compacts for an immediate need, only to trade them in for a roomier car a few months later. **Utilities are making a similar mistake.** They pour billions into battery installations that will age out quickly and offer nowhere near the required capacity for a truly modern electric grid.

Historically, unplanned infrastructure expansions have led to costly errors. For example, the rushed nuclear builds of the 1970s ballooned in expense and created lasting safety issues. Today's rush toward battery storage and everything electric could spawn a new generation of stranded assets, and each installation addresses only a fraction of our surplus energy problem, leaving the rest curtailed or wasted.

We also see a false sense of solution creeping into the industry. Once billions are sunk into battery tech, it becomes harder to pivot to other storage options—even if those alternatives provide better long-term value; this is analogous to building a vast gas-station network only capable of fueling compact cars when we know the demands for trucks, buses, and freight vehicles are much larger.

Mother Nature helps store Hydrogen easily for free in salt caverns:

PROJECT SUMMARY

In June 2022, the Department of Energy issued a $504.4 million loan guarantee to finance Advanced Clean Energy Storage—a clean hydrogen and energy storage facility capable of providing long-term, seasonal energy storage. The facility in Delta, Utah, will combine 220 megawatts of alkaline electrolysis with two massive 4.5 million barrel salt caverns to store clean hydrogen. Advanced Clean Energy Storage will capture excess renewable energy when it is most abundant, store it as hydrogen, then deploy it as fuel for the Intermountain Power Agency's (IPA) IPP Renewed Project—a hydrogen-capable gas turbine and combined cycle power plant that intends to incrementally be fueled by 100 percent clean hydrogen by 2045.

TECHNOLOGY INNOVATION

Advanced Clean Energy Storage uses a 220-megawatt bank of electrolyzers and intermittent renewable energy to produce hydrogen, store it in salt caverns, and deliver that hydrogen for future dispatchable generation.[22] *The scale of deployed electrolyzers and the use of salt caverns to store hydrogen are significant innovations.*

The Case for Hydrogen Storage: Turning Eight Hours into Infinity

Travel across the windy Great Plains, and you'll find a perfect testing ground for hydrogen storage. Instead of capping out after eight hours, hydrogen tanks can expand to hold every electron of surplus energy, whether it's generated at 2 AM or 2 PM, in summer or winter. Each megawatt-hour of curtailed electricity can produce about 20 kilograms of hydrogen—equal to 20 gallons of diesel fuel.

Unlike large battery installations, which degrade over time and require complex cooling, hydrogen can be stored in steel tanks that last for decades. It doesn't demand rare earth metals or rely heavily on foreign supply chains. It can also serve multiple applications: fueling trucks, heating industrial furnaces, and even generating electricity during peak demand.

The kicker is scalability. With hydrogen, adding more storage is as straightforward as adding more tanks or underground caverns; no redesign of the fundamental technology is needed. For states in the center of the country, which often produce more wind energy than they can use, hydrogen conversion could power their service fleets and slash fossil fuel imports. Their current curtailment could produce the equivalent of 140,160,000 gallons of diesel fuel every year.

From Limitation to Liberation: Why America's Energy Future Can't Wait

Our biggest hurdle isn't generating renewable power; it's storing it at scale. Batteries help with short peaks and valleys, but they hit a hard stop after about eight hours. Hydrogen, on the other hand, can store days, weeks, or even months of surplus energy. This is a game-changer for any industrial nation.

Every dollar funneled into undersized battery projects is a missed chance to invest in solutions that address the real scope of our energy needs. Time is short, and demands are growing. By embracing hydrogen, we're not just finding a place to stash extra energy; we're building a flexible, long-term infrastructure that fosters genuine energy independence.

Myth #2: Hydrogen is too hard to store and handle.

A huge benefit of hydrogen is that Mother Nature already supplied us with massive underground storage tanks for hydrogen gas; the cost to build a storage container is eliminated by using underground storage. Essentially, **the cost of hydrogen storage is almost free.** We, as a nation, could produce and store millions of tons of hydrogen underground. By producing hydrogen on-site, we can store it safely and distribute that same hydrogen on-site. Since hydrogen will not be transported, the cost of transportation is *completely* eliminated.

Conclusion for Chapter 4

In Chapter 4, we explored why battery storage alone can't solve our growing surplus energy crisis. Short duration, high replacement costs, foreign supply dependencies, and safety concerns all limit the role of large-scale batteries. Hydrogen, however, offers scalable, long-duration storage that can capture every excess megawatt-hour, convert it into a valuable fuel, and release it whenever needed—days, weeks, or months later. As we'll see in subsequent chapters, it isn't just a theoretical possibility; this technology is a practical and necessary evolution if we want to break our reliance on foreign oil and move toward a cleaner, more stable energy future.

Chapter 5:

Hydrogen: The Universe's Most Abundant Element: Unlocking Nature's Perfect Battery

In my thirty-five years of studying energy solutions, I have learned 1000 different ways hydrogen would not work and would not be cost-effective or profitable. I have also talked to everyone I know about the benefits of hydrogen and how it could solve world problems. And, I have witnessed countless "breakthroughs" promised by scientists, entrepreneurs, and politicians. Yet, the most powerful solution has been with us since the dawn of time—an element so abundant it makes up 75% of the known universe, fuels every star in the galaxy, and combines with oxygen to form the water that flows from our taps.[23] In the previous chapter, we examined the limitations of current battery storage technology. Now we turn to a solution that transcends those constraints. This isn't about inventing something new, it's about recognizing what nature has already perfected: hydrogen.

A recent discussion with a UC Davis student reminded me of the same simple experiment I first conducted in my eighth-grade science class: passing an electric current through water to separate it into hydrogen and oxygen. The simplicity of this process belies its revolutionary potential. These students weren't just splitting water molecules; they were demonstrating a method that could transform America's energy landscape.

What makes hydrogen particularly compelling isn't just its abundance; it is also its versatility. Unlike electricity, which must be used immediately or lost forever, hydrogen can be stored indefinitely. Unlike batteries, which degrade over time, hydrogen maintains its energy potential forever. And, unlike fossil fuels, which release greenhouse gases when burned, hydrogen's only emission is water vapor. Its beauty lies in the complete, sustainable cycle: solar panels and wind turbines capture energy, which is then used to split water into hydrogen and oxygen. The hydrogen can be stored until needed, then recombined with oxygen in a fuel cell to produce electricity and water—completing a perfectly clean energy loop.[24]

This isn't science fiction or a distant dream. The technology exists today, proven through decades of real-world use—from NASA space shuttle missions to industrial processes. The missing piece is not the technology. The missing piece is recognizing that we already have a scalable solution to our energy storage challenges. As we'll see, hydrogen isn't just another energy technology. It is nature's perfect battery, capable of storing massive amounts of energy without degradation. From powering heavy-duty trucks to stabilizing our electrical grid and enabling true energy independence, hydrogen addresses challenges that have long seemed insurmountable.

Demystifying Hydrogen Production: It's Not Rocket Science (Though Rockets Use It Too)

When I visited Joseph Gallo Farms in California's Central Valley, I witnessed something remarkable: a cheese-making facility that turned dairy waste into a power generation system producing electricity, heat, and steam, all from biogas or "cow poop".[25] Watching this integrated energy system at work made me realize that if we can convert dairy waste into energy, imagine what we could do with the enormous amounts of human waste which could be converted to electricity and hydrogen fuel.

This is where hydrogen production enters the picture. The process is simpler than most people realize. Think back to basic chemistry: H2O—two hydrogen atoms bonded to one oxygen atom. Through electrolysis, electricity splits water into its component parts. The technology for electrolysis hasn't fundamentally changed since its discovery in 1789.[26] What has changed is our ability to do it at scale and our urgent need for large-scale energy storage.

Hydrogen production requires remarkably little water. Producing 1 kilogram of hydrogen—enough to power a heavy-duty truck for many miles—takes 9-11 liters of water.[27] This is roughly the same amount needed to produce a single almond. Moreover, the water isn't really used up. It is transformed into hydrogen and oxygen, eventually recombined into water again in the fuel cell process. It can even be sourced from pond water, seawater, or atmospheric moisture. We aren't depleting water resources. We're simply converting water into an energy carrier and returning it later.

The production process itself is clean and quiet. Unlike the complex systems required for oil refining or natural gas processing, which cause greenhouse gases and toxic fumes in the air. The good news about electrolysis is that it has no moving parts. Water and electricity go in, and hydrogen and oxygen come out. No smoke, no noise, no harmful emissions. Meanwhile, the byproduct—pure oxygen—can be captured and sold for medical or industrial uses.

One of hydrogen's greatest advantages is that it can be produced exactly where it's needed. Unlike massive oil refineries that demand large safety zones, hydrogen production units can be scaled to fit various applications. A warehouse can install an electrolyzer to power forklifts; a trucking company can generate hydrogen at its distribution center; a farm can create its own fuel using solar panels and wind turbines to power its tractors and whole farming operation. This distributed model eliminates the common criticism about transporting hydrogen over long distances. By creating a closed-loop system, we gain both efficiency and security.

Five Sources of Clean Energy: Nature's Power Portfolio

During discussions with my brother, Ron, a retired utility executive living in Iowa's wind belt, he told me a common misconception: green hydrogen production must rely solely on solar and wind. The reality is far more diverse. Like a balanced investment portfolio, green hydrogen can draw from five distinct renewable sources, each with unique advantages.

1. **Biomass (Humanity's Oldest Energy Source)**

   At a lumber mill in Jamestown, California, I watched waste wood—sawdust and wood chips that would otherwise be discarded—being used to generate clean power. Biomass includes agricultural waste, forest residues, and urban wood waste. Every city, farm, and forest contains potential energy waiting to be harnessed for hydrogen production.

2. **Hydropower (Clean and Consistent)**

   Standing atop the Hoover Dam, I witnessed millions of gallons of water flowing through turbines to produce electricity. Hydropower has been operating for nearly a century and provides a steady 24/7 power output—ideal for continuous hydrogen production. Unlike solar or wind, it doesn't depend on weather conditions or time of day.

3. **Biogas (Turning Waste into Wealth)**

   Across America, the thousands of wastewater treatment plants could all produce electricity during peak hours and hydrogen gas when not needed.[28] Also, landfills and dairy farms produce methane that's often flared or released into the atmosphere. Capturing and using this biogas to generate electricity for electrolysis transforms waste into a valuable resource. If every city harnessed the methane from its sewage plant, the hydrogen output would be substantial. The best part about biogas and hydrogen is that we solve three problems with one conversion: get rid of toxic waste, produce electricity during peak times, and produce hydrogen when electricity is not needed.

4. **Solar (From Rooftops to Utility-Scale Farms)**

   Solar energy has soared in popularity and affordability. From vast utility-scale installations to rooftop panels, solar can generate electricity during peak daylight hours, oftentimes when the grid doesn't need it all. Converting that excess into hydrogen prevents wasting valuable electrons.

5. **Wind (Harvesting the Invisible Resource)**

   In the Midwest, farmers are discovering they can grow corn and harvest wind energy simultaneously. When wind turbines generate power beyond immediate grid demand, that surplus can be used for electrolysis—turning wind power into storable, dispatchable hydrogen.

What makes this "portfolio approach" so effective is the complementary nature of these sources. When the sun isn't shining, the wind may be blowing. When the wind is calm, hydropower can fill the gap. Seasonal variations that affect one source can be balanced by another. This redundancy isn't just about backup—it's about creating resilience.

Moreover, these are proven technologies, not futuristic concepts. The real innovation lies in connecting them to hydrogen production, forming a flexible, scalable system that can store energy from any excess electricity source. Every region of America—deserts, coastlines, agricultural areas, mountainous regions—can contribute its own excess renewable resources to a nationwide hydrogen economy. By tapping into all five sources, no community or state is left out. No energy goes to waste, and our clean energy revolution gains real momentum.

The Promise Fulfilled: Making Hydrogen the Cornerstone of American Energy Independence

Throughout this chapter, we've seen how hydrogen—the universe's most abundant element—can transform America's energy landscape. From the simplicity of electrolysis to the five diverse sources of green and, in some cases, ***free power***, the roadmap to a hydrogen-powered future is already before us. The real strength of hydrogen lies in its capacity to reshape our entire relationship with energy; it is all around us.

Visualize a hydrogen-based system where excess solar and wind power in Texas is converted into hydrogen that fuels trucking fleets across the Southwest. Or, imagine wind energy in the Great Plains harnessed during off-peak hours to power industrial facilities at a later time. Biogas from California's dairy farms could supply agricultural equipment and food processing. Biogas could also be produced at the 16,800 wastewater treatment plants. Then they can use that hydrogen to power street sweepers and garbage trucks. By uniting renewable energy sources under one flexible storage and distribution medium, our grid becomes more efficient, reliable, and resilient.

Hydrogen isn't merely about replacing one fuel with another. It's about creating an entirely new energy ecosystem. Rather than wasting surplus renewable power, we store it until it's needed when demand starts to peak. Instead of letting that power go to waste, we transform it into a long-lasting, dispatchable energy resource. The cycle is as simple as eighth-grade chemistry: split water, store hydrogen, and recombine it with oxygen when needed. Nature has run this cycle for billions of years. We're just catching up.

Safety, once a top concern, has been thoroughly addressed. Modern hydrogen systems have passed rigorous tests—crashes, bullet impacts, extreme temperatures—and it's proven safer than all other liquid fuels.[29] When handled responsibly, hydrogen disperses quickly in the event of a leak, reducing the risk of catastrophic fire. The infamous Hindenburg disaster is often referenced. Yet, its main hazard was the airship's flammable skin coating, not the hydrogen within.[30]

As we progress toward Chapter 5, we'll dive deeper into how technical potential translates into financial reality. We already know hydrogen works. The key now is to finance and scale these systems in ways that make sense for utilities, businesses, and consumers. With renewable energy curtailment on the rise and technological costs dropping, the economic case for hydrogen is stronger than ever.

The next step is aligning financial incentives and regulations to speed up this shift. Utilities can convert wasted renewable energy into valuable fuel; trucking companies can produce their own clean power; industrial facilities can generate both electricity and process heat—all using the same hydrogen system. This isn't just a shift in how we power our economy. It's a transformation of the economy itself.

The technology is here. The resources are abundant. The need is pressing. All that remains is the will and wisdom to deploy it. Hydrogen—powering our sun and forming our oceans—is ready to power our future. The question now is whether we're ready to seize the opportunity.

Conclusion for Chapter 5

Hydrogen stands out as nature's perfect battery: abundant, flexible, and clean. This chapter has shown how electrolysis can transform water into a storable energy carrier and how multiple renewable sources—from biomass to wind—can supply electricity for hydrogen production. We've seen how hydrogen's versatility can reshape our energy ecosystem, turning today's wasted electricity into tomorrow's wealth and ensuring no electrons go unused. As we look ahead, the real work involves scaling this proven technology to meet our energy demands, aligning financial incentives, and embracing a more decentralized, resilient grid. Hydrogen isn't a distant dream. It's a practical, powerful solution already within reach. It will be the cornerstone of true **American Energy Dominance.**

Chapter 6:

The Next Gold Rush

How Hydrogen Will Spark America's Next Economic Revolution

The universe's most abundant element isn't just a solution to our energy needs. It's poised to unleash an economic transformation that could rival the discovery of oil itself. While the technical capabilities of hydrogen are well-established (as discussed in the previous chapter), it's the financial revolution behind hydrogen that will ultimately drive widespread adoption and reshape America's energy future.

Picture this: every day across the country, utility companies pay others to take excess electricity off their hands. It's comparable to a farmer paying someone to haul away perfectly good crops or a manufacturer paying to dispose of finished products. In California alone, over three gigawatt-hours of green electricity are curtailed annually.[31] That's enough to produce around 60,000 kilograms of hydrogen—energy that's already been paid for, simply going to waste.

Where some see waste, visionaries see opportunity. Just as the early oil barons recognized petroleum's transformative potential, today's energy pioneers are positioning themselves at the forefront of a new hydrogen economy. Unlike the oil boom—where wealth was concentrated in a few hands, and America grew dependent on foreign powers—this hydrogen revolution has the potential to democratize energy production while keeping profits circulating through American communities.

Consider the early days of wind energy in Iowa: farmers who once struggled with fluctuating crop prices suddenly enjoyed steady income from turbine leases. The hydrogen revolution promises similar opportunities on an even greater scale. Every region with surplus renewable energy—from the windy plains of Kansas to the sun-baked deserts of Nevada—could become a hub for producing clean hydrogen from resources that would otherwise be curtailed.

One megawatt-hour of electricity can produce enough 20 kilograms of hydrogen to power a semi-truck for hundreds of miles.[32] When that electricity is essentially free because it otherwise would have been wasted, the economics become irresistible; this isn't about marginal improvements. It's about transforming discarded energy into a valuable commodity while tackling our energy independence challenges head-on.

In the pages ahead, we'll explore why this financial revolution is already unfolding: from the clever funding mechanisms that spark initial adoption to the long-term economic benefits that will reshape our communities. We'll review real-world case studies, analyze the numbers that make hydrogen compelling, and show why savvy investors have already begun positioning themselves for the greatest energy shift of the century.

The age of foreign oil dependence is waning. In its place, a new American energy economy is emerging: cleaner, more equitable, and more profitable than anything we've seen before. We can spread the profit across the American landscape to many industries. The only question is who will seize the opportunity first.

Breaking the Cost Barrier: Why Hydrogen's Economics Finally Make Sense

For decades, critics labeled hydrogen too expensive. Infrastructure costs seemed prohibitive, and the math didn't pencil out when electricity prices were high. This information is based on 50 years ago. It is like comparing IBM computers from the '60s to today's cell phones. Times have changed. With the rapid expansion of solar and wind farms, people installing solar on their homes, and the frequent curtailment of this energy, today's circumstances have fundamentally shifted hydrogen's cost equation.

A host of factors now make hydrogen both environmentally and financially sustainable, as well as hugely profitable.

You've already paid for the curtailed electricity. Rather than letting that paid-for energy vanish, converting it into hydrogen creates value. Every kilogram produced reduces grid management costs. Every service vehicle converted to hydrogen removes the volatility of diesel prices. Having hydrogen storage on-site allows all electric installations to run at peak efficiency, even if immediate demand is low.

Traditional cost analyses often focus on the per-kilogram production cost of hydrogen versus diesel. That's a narrow lens. A broader look reveals how hydrogen addresses negative pricing periods, avoids costly grid upgrades, generates multiple revenue streams, and reduces fuel price risk. Factor in the steady advances in electrolyzer technology and fuel-cell efficiency (which keeps dropping in price just like computers did 30 years ago), and hydrogen becomes even more attractive.[33]

This isn't a distant possibility—it's happening now. Utilities and fleet operators across the country are becoming aware that hydrogen can outperform traditional fuels from a bottom-line perspective. The returns are immediate and tangible: stable fuel prices, profits from what used to be wasted energy, and a competitive edge over businesses still reliant on volatile diesel markets.

Financing the Future: How Wall Street Is Quietly Betting on Hydrogen

The math is compelling. Envision a medium-sized utility company like Comcast or AT&T, with 1,000 service vehicles using 200 gallons of fuel per month. In California, at the current gas price of $5.00 per gallon, they may spend around $12 million annually on fuel—that's about $12,000 per truck. By capturing curtailed energy and converting it into hydrogen, the company could drastically reduce or even eliminate that fuel expense. Upfront infrastructure costs are recouped relatively quickly. After they're effectively producing fuel from what was once waste. All that they would need to do is negotiate the price for hydrogen.

This fundamental restructuring of energy economics has not gone unnoticed by major financial institutions. The United States currently imports over six million barrels of oil a day at around $70 per barrel. That is $420 million a day. That is easily an annual expenditure of over $150 billion, flowing out of the domestic economy every year.[34] Even redirecting a fraction of those dollars into local hydrogen production represents one of the largest economic opportunities in generations.

Financing models are evolving to meet the moment. Banks and private equity firms are developing hydrogen-as-a-service packages, funding the entire buildout in exchange for a per-kilogram fee. Others create special-purpose vehicles, allowing multiple fleet operators to share infrastructure costs. Such creative structures remove the biggest obstacle—upfront capital—making hydrogen adoption viable for municipal fleets and mid-sized electric generating companies.

Wall Street's message is clear: hydrogen isn't just another green-energy fad. It's a transformative economic pivot. With the energy industry's gross revenue going off the charts, reaching over $1 trillion, don't you think Wall Street will be financing this revolution?[35] The question is less about whether hydrogen will become part of America's energy backbone and more about who stands to profit the most from its inevitable rise.

Building the New Energy Economy: From Main Street to Wall Street

This revolution isn't restricted to big corporations or Silicon Valley investors. Take, for example, Three Rivers Electric Co-op, a modest electricity cooperative in Nebraska. Initially, they felt left out as large-scale wind farms dotted their horizon. With most of their profits going to major energy companies, they were unable to profit from the wind curtailment. Then, they decided to use curtailed wind energy to produce hydrogen for their service fleet and supplied hydrogen gas to the local pork processing plant, which used hydrogen to heat water and produce electricity for their operation. With grants from the Department of Agriculture and local bank financing, they installed a small electrolyzer and a storage tank. What began as a fuel-cost savings measure quickly evolved into a revenue generator as the pork processor expanded by using hydrogen to power their forklifts. Within eighteen months, the co-op had a brand-new income stream.

Such examples could easily pop up across the country. Rural electric cooperatives realize they have land and infrastructure connections in regions with surplus wind, solar, or conventional power. By producing hydrogen from otherwise wasted energy, they add a local, profitable revenue source while supporting community jobs. When dollars stay local, they build schools, roads, and other public services rather than sending money overseas for oil.

This democratization of energy represents a profound shift. America's energy sources have long been centralized—controlled by a small number of corporate giants and foreign producers. Hydrogen flips the script: any area with surplus renewables or conventional power can produce fuel, reducing dependence on outside sources. Meanwhile, local contractors install systems, local banks finance projects, and local fleets cut fuel costs. It's an economic revival from the ground up.

Running the Numbers: A Practical Guide to Hydrogen Economics

Traditional studies compared hydrogen to diesel on a strict cost-per-kilogram basis, failing to account for wider benefits. So, I have developed a five-point metric that changes the conversation:

1. **Fuel Cost Stability**

   Hydrogen contracts often offer fixed pricing for years, eliminating hedging costs and insulating operations from oil price shocks. If you are an electricity producer, your fuel cost could plummet because the cost of electricity would be minimal.

2. **Vehicle Longevity**

   Fuel-cell trucks have fewer moving parts and typically last longer than diesel trucks, effectively stretching capital investments.

3. **Maintenance Savings**

   No oil changes, fewer filters, and no complex emissions systems lower cost and downtime. No transmissions, no engines, fewer breakdowns.

4. **Infrastructure Phasing**

   Instead of building a massive electrolyzer from day one, the co-op team began with a modest system sized to their initial conversion goal; this minimized stranded assets.

5. **Future-Proofing**

   Hydrogen fleets face fewer restrictions in regions imposing diesel bans or low-emission mandates, creating a strategic advantage over competitors still reliant on diesel.

Even with higher initial costs, the co-op was on track to break even in just a couple of years. After that, every month of operation represented pure financial advantage. This case is not unique. More companies are discovering that a holistic analysis of hydrogen projects reveals compelling business logic, not just environmental gains.

Making It Happen: A Strategic Framework for Implementation

The gap between recognizing an opportunity and capitalizing on it can be immense. Success hinges on starting small, phasing in projects, and leveraging existing assets rather than trying to do everything overnight.

Central Valley Power & Light, a small utility company, serves as an example of what could happen by converting excess electricity to hydrogen. They identified that 40% of their service vehicles operated predictable routes, returning to the same yards nightly, making them ideal for a pilot hydrogen program. By focusing on these vehicles:

1. They **matched supply with demand** by producing only as much hydrogen as their pilot fleet required.
2. They **leveraged existing infrastructure**, installing an electrolyzer at a service yard with high-capacity electrical connections.
3. They **phased their rollout** to coincide with the normal replacement cycle of aging vehicles, minimizing sunk costs.

4. They **captured multiple revenue streams**, designing the system to eventually sell surplus hydrogen to other fleets.

Within eight months, Central Valley Power & Light converted 20 trucks, slashed fuel costs, and created an entirely new revenue channel. The lesson is clear: hydrogen success doesn't demand untested technology. It demands smart planning, strategic partnerships, and a willingness to view waste as an opportunity.

The Financial Revolution Is Already Here

Throughout this chapter, we've seen how hydrogen production can transform financial liabilities into assets—turning waste into profit and shifting energy production from global to local. Redirecting even a fraction of the $150+ billion spent on foreign oil every year into domestic hydrogen projects has enormous potential to boost local economies and enhance national security.

This transition is also remarkably accessible. Hydrogen systems can be scaled to serve a single rural co-op or an entire municipal fleet. As improvements in electrolyzer technology drive down costs, and as more utilities realize they're paying for electricity they can't sell, hydrogen's value proposition gets stronger. We're already witnessing the ripple effects: major banks are setting up specialized funds for all of renewable energy, insurers are crafting hydrogen-friendly policies, and private equity firms are eyeing and can't wait to **invest in this transforming industry.**

Most important is hydrogen's democratizing effect on energy production. No longer does a region need to sit on oil fields to profit from the energy market. Solar in Arizona, wind in the Central Plains, biomass in the South, and hydroelectric in the Pacific Northwest can all be tapped to create hydrogen locally, fueling trucks, buses, and fleets that once ran on foreign oil. Every kilogram of hydrogen produced domestically is another step toward true energy independence.

The tools exist. The technology is proven. The financial models work. The revolution in energy economics isn't coming—it's here.

Conclusion for Chapter 6

Hydrogen's economic promise is clear. It allows us to transform surplus renewable energy into a valuable commodity, cut fuel costs for fleets, stabilize energy pricing, and keep billions of dollars circulating in local communities. Whether you're a small co-op, a municipal fleet manager, or a major investor, hydrogen offers a path to both environmental responsibility and financial gain. The initiatives outlined in this chapter—everything from phased rollouts to flexible financing models—demonstrate that what was once considered a futuristic idea is already becoming a mainstream reality.

In short, **the next gold rush is here, and it's powered by hydrogen.** By transforming curtailed energy into clean fuel, we aren't just solving an environmental challenge—we're igniting a homegrown economic revolution that benefits everyone, from Main Street to Wall Street.

Chapter 7:

Rewriting the Supply Chain—How Hydrogen Will Bring Energy Production Back Home

Every day, a massive fleet of oil tankers crosses the world's oceans. Thousands of these colossal ships burn millions of gallons of diesel fuel to transport oil that will, ironically, be burned again as fuel.[36] Each vessel emits pollution, each transfer point risks an environmental accident, and every mile traveled adds cost and complexity to a global supply chain that often spans halfway around the world.

This is the reality of America's current energy infrastructure—a system so convoluted and inefficient it would be laughable if it weren't so costly. We burn fossil fuels to find more fossil fuels, use extra fuel to extract them, still more to ship them, and then even more to refine them. At each step, energy is wasted and burned, giving off toxic fumes. The financial toll of this dependency is staggering, but the implications for our supply chain and security are perhaps even greater.

Now, a different reality is possible: energy production that happens just miles from where it's needed, using "raw material" that falls from the sky as rain or flows through our rivers. Picture a production process whose only byproduct is oxygen, with underground storage (salt caverns) and distribution taking place on a local scale. In such a world, jobs stay in the community, and our energy security no longer hinges on precarious global routes or overseas markets.

This isn't a utopian dream—it's the vision that hydrogen power makes possible. By radically simplifying the supply chain, hydrogen can eliminate layers of waste and strengthen U.S. energy security. Our current system relies on a highly orchestrated, global symphony of shipping, multiple refinement steps, and supply lines vulnerable to regional conflicts and other disruptions. *A hydrogen-based supply chain can be as simple as water, surplus electricity, and smart storage*, of which we have an abundance of all three. In this chapter, we'll explore how this revolution is already taking shape across America—and how it might create opportunities for everyone from local businesses to national security planners.

From Global Chaos to Local Control: Reimagining Energy Distribution

Consider the journey of a single gallon of gasoline from an oil field in Saudi Arabia. First, it's pumped using diesel-fueled equipment. Then, transported via pipeline or truck to a coastal terminal, using more fuel. Next, it's loaded onto a tanker that might burn around 60,000 gallons of marine fuel per day on its weeks-long voyage to America. Once it arrives, more energy is used to offload it. Then it's piped or trucked to a refinery (burning more fuel again), refined (requiring still more energy), and finally shipped to local filling stations.

Not only is this supply chain staggeringly inefficient, but it's also highly vulnerable. One blocked canal or regional conflict in the Middle East can disrupt the flow of oil, sending shockwaves through the economy. Every additional handoff and mile represents extra cost, greater risk, and higher pollution.

Now contrast that with hydrogen's potential supply chain of tomorrow: local water sources, local electricity, local storage, and local distribution. No oil tankers crossing oceans. No worrying about foreign obstructions. No complicated refining. No semi-trucks full of gasoline are traveling down the highway like one big bomb. The "raw materials" are all around us: abundant water, surplus electricity, and salt cavern storage.

Localizing energy production also creates local jobs. Instead of sending billions of dollars abroad to support oil exploration, extraction, shipping, and refining, communities can invest those dollars in hydrogen production, storage, maintenance, and distribution. With more control over energy resources, a region becomes more resilient to global disruptions and more responsive to local needs.

Building the Hydrogen Highway: Infrastructure for the New Energy Economy

When the United States first embarked on the interstate highway system, many doubted it could ever be fully built or maintained. Yet, the finished network transformed the country's economy. Skeptics raise similar concerns about "hydrogen highways" today, but history shows that well-planned infrastructure can spark sweeping change.

Critically important, we're not starting from zero. America's electrical grid, though in need of upgrades, already provides a foundation for hydrogen production. Each utility substation, renewable energy facility, and industrial park with high-capacity power lines could be a potential hydrogen hub. The real challenge is strategically adding production and storage to meet demand, not rebuilding everything from the ground up.

For instance, one Pacific Northwest utility decided to locate a hydrogen "hub" right next to a major substation along a freight corridor. Because the utility already had strong electrical connections, existing security, and the land, building this station cost less than a standard gas station. They started by fueling their fleet, ensuring immediate demand. Over time, as local trucking companies recognized the benefits, demand naturally grew, solving the classic "chicken and egg" problem that alternative fuel systems often face.

Building hydrogen infrastructure boils down to five elements:

1. Power supply (utilities already have this)
2. Water supply (readily available in most locations)
3. Electrolysis equipment (modular and scalable)
4. Storage tanks (familiar, proven technology)
5. Dispensing equipment (similar to gas stations)

All of these are well-established technologies. The key is deploying them wisely. Instead of massive, centralized facilities serving huge areas, a more distributed approach allows communities to add capacity incrementally, matching local demand.

The Role of Utilities: From Power Providers to Energy Revolutionaries

Shifting to a hydrogen-powered future doesn't just change how we produce and transport fuel—it also redefines the mission of utility companies. Traditionally, utilities have generated electricity, pushed it across the grid, and billed customers by the kilowatt-hour. Hydrogen now gives them the chance to become orchestrators of energy independence.

Midwest Power Cooperative offers a good example of what could happen. Facing frequent curtailment, they sometimes had to shut down 40% of their wind turbines, wasting electricity they'd already paid to produce. Installing hydrogen production capacity turned that waste into opportunity: every curtailed megawatt became hydrogen that could power heavy trucks for miles.

By placing hydrogen production facilities throughout their service area, the co-op transformed localities into "energy independence zones." Communities no longer relied on oil shipped across oceans; instead, they used surplus wind power to run buses, trucks, and even backup generators. In this new paradigm, utilities don't just sell electricity. They also supply clean transportation fuel, energy storage, backup power, and more.

This evolution is beneficial for both utilities and their customers. Utilities already have infrastructure, distribution rights-of-way, and deep knowledge of local demand. Expanding into hydrogen lets them tap new revenue streams and stabilize the grid. Meanwhile, local residents and businesses gain a stable, eco-friendly energy supply that circulates money and jobs and frees us from foreign oil.

Matching Supply with Demand: The Art of Energy Orchestration

One of hydrogen's greatest advantages is its flexibility in matching local supply and demand. Traditional energy systems often struggle with seasonal peaks, like an agricultural town in Iowa needing power for harvest or a ski resort in Colorado surging during the winter months. Hydrogen, produced and stored on-site, allows for far more precise control.

A transit authority in the Rocky Mountains illustrates this concept. Their bus fleet has enormous demand spikes in summer when tourism is high, but much lower activity in the off-season. They installed a modest hydrogen production facility for the peak summer months, and when demand dropped, the same production capacity could be redirected for local delivery fleets, backup power, and industrial needs.

Planners often call this demand stacking. One hydrogen production facility can serve multiple uses, improving overall economics and resilience. Instead of siloed systems for different energy needs, communities can develop integrated solutions:

- Municipal and emergency fleets
- Local trucking corridors
- Industrial processes
- Grid-level energy storage

Each case boosts economic viability, creating a more robust local energy ecosystem. The region keeps energy spending close to home, spurring development in maintenance, distribution, and related services.

The Dawn of America's Energy Revolution

Hydrogen offers an opportunity to replace a vulnerable global supply chain with resilient local systems. Rather than spending billions each year on foreign oil imports, communities can invest in homegrown energy solutions. Instead of relying on worldwide shipping lanes prone to conflict or disaster, we can build self-sufficient local networks.

This transition doesn't require reinventing the wheel. The electrical grid, water resources, and existing hydrogen storage demonstrate that much of the necessary infrastructure is already in place. It's more a matter of reorganizing our approach—of focusing on localized production, flexible storage, and incremental expansion that aligns with real-world demand.

When communities become energy producers, they keep jobs and dollars circulating locally. They gain career paths in hydrogen production, infrastructure maintenance, and distribution—jobs that can't be outsourced overseas. Meanwhile, each successful hydrogen project offers a blueprint for other regions to follow, gradually weaving a national tapestry of energy independence.

In the chapters ahead, you'll see how this simpler, more secure supply chain is already fueling the fleet revolution, starting with buses, trucks, and municipal vehicles that log predictable, centralized routes. These fleets represent an ideal proving ground for the broader shift toward hydrogen-powered transportation. Early results suggest it's not only doable but profitable— financially and environmentally.

Conclusion for Chapter 7

Hydrogen has the potential to completely rewrite America's energy supply chain. By harnessing local water and electricity to produce a clean, versatile fuel, we can shrink our dependence on foreign oil, create jobs in our communities, and significantly reduce environmental risks. Utilities become pivotal players in this evolution, transforming from mere power providers to full-scale energy innovators. Through a distributed network of hydrogen hubs, we match production to demand and ensure resilience even in the face of global disruptions. In short, hydrogen is not just another fuel choice—it's a chance to build a more self-reliant, responsive, and profitable energy future for all.

Chapter 8:

The Fleet Revolution

Introduction: Finding Our "Big W"

After examining America's hydrogen transition—particularly the infrastructure needs and the role of utilities—one crucial question remains: **where do we start?** The answer is right under our noses, much like Jimmy Durante's "Big W" in *It's a Mad, Mad, Mad, Mad World.* While everyone was searching for a secret clue hidden among four palm trees, only the young girl who wasn't looking for the W spotted it first.

That "Big W" for us is the trucks running up and down our highways each day. Medium and heavy-duty trucks account for nearly **29% of all harmful emissions (CIT)** in the United States.[37] These workhorses shuttle between distribution centers, haul materials to construction sites, collect waste, and keep our cities running. They're also the easiest segment to convert to hydrogen power, with technology that is **ready to roll now**—not in a decade, not as a moonshot, but **today**.

Why fleets first? Because the manufacturers (Ford, General Motors, Dodge, Freightliner, Kenworth, etc.) already know how to build great trucks. All that's changing is swapping out the diesel engine for a hydrogen fuel cell powertrain with electric motors (changing out the drivetrain). From the outside, they'll look exactly like the trucks we know, but instead of coughing out diesel fumes, they'll emit water vapor.

Think about a utility company like Pacific Gas & Electric (PG&E) with a fleet of 14,000 service vehicles. They're paying a fortune in diesel costs every day, and at the same time, paying others to take their excess electricity. **With hydrogen, they could use that curtailed electricity to power their entire fleet, turning waste into profit.** They have wasted fuel. They could easily build these hydrogen fueling depots in the yard where they park their trucks at night. No need for expensive upgrades. They just need the Fuel Cell Electric Truck and the electrolyzer hydrogen plant. That's a solution hiding in plain sight.

The best part? PG&E already knows exactly how many miles these trucks drive, what routes they take, and how much fuel they use. This is **simple math**, not wishful thinking. And, unlike battery-electric vehicles, hydrogen trucks can refuel in minutes and carry full payloads without sacrificing range.[38]

This chapter lays out the practical roadmap for transforming America's commercial fleets. We're not waiting on some future miracle technology. We're not betting on a massive infrastructure overhaul before we can begin. **The trucks exist. The fuel cells exist. And we are throwing away the electricity needed to power them.**

Understanding Fuel Cell Electric Trucks: A Revolution Hidden in Plain Sight

Much like Henry Ford revolutionized transportation by making cars affordable for the average American, we're standing at a similar crossroads with hydrogen-powered trucks. The good news is that today, **this isn't experimental**; Toyota, Freightliner, and just about all car and truck manufacturers have a hydrogen-powered prototype. Others have already proven the concept with real trucks on real roads.

So, how do these trucks work?[39] Instead of a diesel engine, there's a **fuel cell** acting like a mini power plant. It combines hydrogen (stored in tanks mounted behind or underneath the cab) with oxygen from the air. This reaction generates electricity to power the truck's electric motors and to charge the batteries, emitting **only water vapor**.

Driving a Fuel Cell Electric Truck (FCET) is strikingly similar to driving a traditional truck—actually, it's **easier** because there's no shifting. They're also **much quieter**. When I test-drove a Toyota fuel cell vehicle on Interstate 80, the loudest sound at 80 miles per hour was the air conditioning. For drivers, that means less fatigue and more comfort.

Hydrogen trucks solve problems battery-electric trucks can't. For a Class 8 semi-truck to travel 500 miles using a battery-electric system, you'd need thousands of pounds of batteries, leaving little payload capacity. With hydrogen, you get the same range with hydrogen storage tanks weighing just a fraction of what a battery semi truck would need to move any sizable load. You will be able to haul as much as a diesel truck. With refueling, it's as quick as filling up a diesel tank—just a few minutes at the pump, and you're back on the road.

Maintenance is **simpler** too: fewer moving parts, no oil changes, no complex transmissions, and no exhaust after-treatment systems. Brakes last longer because of regenerative braking. The trucks themselves can often be refurbished with upgraded fuel cell stacks instead of being replaced outright, meaning a longer vehicle lifespan.

With states like California mandating zero-emission commercial fleets, hydrogen stands out as a solution that **works** in the real world—no range anxiety, no hours-long charging, and no diminishing payload capacity. It's a straightforward technology that eliminates emissions, saves on maintenance, and cuts dependence on foreign oil.

The Real World Math: Why Fleet Managers Are Taking Notice

Fleet managers care about **numbers**, not theories. Picture a company with 100 Class 8 trucks, each burning through 20,000 gallons of diesel per year. At around $5.50 per gallon (typical in parts of California), that's over $11 million in annual fuel costs.

Hydrogen can match diesel mileage on a kilogram-for-gallon diesel fuel basis. Advantageously, hydrogen produced from **curtailed electricity** can cost far less than diesel, especially when you factor in routine diesel price spikes. That means locking in fuel costs for years and avoiding the roller-coaster of international oil prices.

Maintenance savings sweeten the deal. Diesel engines require regular oil changes, filters, exhaust system maintenance, and more. Fuel cells eliminate a lot of that complexity.

Another overlooked advantage is **residual value**. Hydrogen trucks can be refurbished instead of replaced. Swap in a new fuel cell stack after several years and keep rolling with the same chassis, saving huge capital costs over the vehicle's lifetime.

The Infrastructure Advantage: Why Fleets Are the Perfect Starting Point

One reason passenger electric vehicles have faced an uphill battle is the **massive charging infrastructure** required nationwide. Hydrogen fleets don't have that problem: **fleets operate on predictable routes**, returning to central depots nightly. Install hydrogen production and fueling at a single depot, and you can power an entire fleet from one location.

Companies like UPS or FedEx already employ a **hub-and-spoke** model: trucks leave a central hub, do their routes, and come back. Adding a hydrogen station at that hub lets you serve all the trucks without building an entire coast-to-coast network first.

Over time, these hub stations can grow into corridors along major freight routes—take, for example, Interstate 80 across the Midwest. There's so much curtailed wind energy there that it could power thousands of trucks. Setting up fueling hubs at truck stops or distribution centers near the interstate would effectively create a "hydrogen highway" powered by what's now wasted electricity. This is so simple to install at existing truck centers.

Instead of expensive, large-scale national rollouts, each fleet can build or buy into *just enough* infrastructure to meet its needs. Electrolyzers (which split water into hydrogen) are modular and easy to scale. Storage tanks can be incrementally added. The fueling process is similar to CNG (compressed natural gas), a technology many fleets already know. As more fleets switch, economies of scale drive costs down for everyone.

Building the Business Case: From Pilot to Full Fleet Conversion

The best way to start is with a **pilot program**: 5 to 10 trucks running on predictable routes. This allows you to gather real-world data on fuel consumption, maintenance intervals, and costs. You'll see exactly how many kilograms of hydrogen you burn per day, how it performs on hills, or how quickly drivers adapt.

For example, Foster Farms could run a small fleet on a 70-mile route from Livingston to a Safeway warehouse in Tracy, California. They'd set up a single hydrogen station, possibly producing fuel from **their biomass** or curtailed electricity. The loads, schedules, and routes stay the same, only the fuel changes.

Once you have your data—and see the cost savings and reliability improvements for yourself—**scaling up** becomes straightforward. You're not flying blind. You know your cost per mile, daily fuel needs, maintenance intervals, and payback period. The more trucks you convert, the better the economics get.

Since hydrogen trucks have fewer parts to maintain, they can stay on the road longer than diesel trucks. Spread those savings across a 100-vehicle fleet, and you start seeing real profits, not just operational cost avoidance. That's why so many fleets are looking beyond pilot programs to plan **full fleet conversions** in the coming years.

Taking Action: How to Start Your Fleet's Hydrogen Journey Today

Let's get practical. First, **map your routes**: find the trucks that travel predictable paths and end up at the same depot each night. These are your low-hanging fruit. Next, **audit your energy sources**. Are you a utility with curtailed energy? Great—you've already got free fuel. If you're a private fleet operator, talk to your local utility; many are swimming in excess power they'd love to offload.

Then, **connect with truck manufacturers**: Ford, Freightliner, and Kenworth—most have hydrogen truck options or pilot programs available. Take a test drive. See how the truck fits your existing operations, including refueling times and payload capacity.

Infrastructure is simpler than it sounds. Companies like **Cummins** and **Plug Power** offer modular electrolyzers that match your fleet size. Fueling equipment is similar to CNG, and you can start small with just enough for your pilot fleet.

Yes, the upfront cost is higher than diesel, but consider the immediate operational savings: less fuel volatility, lower maintenance, longer truck lifespans, and (often) generous grants or incentives that can offset initial investment. With a well-planned pilot, you'll gather the hard data to justify scaling up.

Success Stories: Real Fleets Making the Hydrogen Transition

You don't have to take anyone's word for it—let's look at real fleets doing this right now:

- **Toyota's Project Portal at the Port of Los Angeles**: Hydrogen trucks are hauling the same containers, climbing the same ramps, and running the same schedules as diesel rigs—just without the emissions.
- A Northern California **food distribution company** uses hydrogen trucks with refrigerated trailers, eliminating the need for a separate diesel generator.
- **Waste management** operators like Republic Services are testing hydrogen for trash collection, a demanding start-stop application that benefits from the instant torque of electric motors.
- **Utility companies** (e.g., Southern California Edison) run service trucks on hydrogen produced by their otherwise wasted electricity.

All these fleets started small, proved the concept, and are scaling up based on **real-world numbers**. They're not chasing some elusive futuristic technology; they're deploying proven solutions that save money, reduce downtime, and clear the air.

Leading America to Energy Independence

The move to hydrogen-powered fleets is more than a green initiative—it's a major **step toward ending our dependence on foreign oil**. Commercial fleets are some of the biggest consumers of diesel. By converting them to hydrogen, we build an infrastructure foundation that can eventually support passenger cars, trains, ships, and more.

Constructively, **we're using domestic energy**—excess wind, solar, or biomass-based power, and all curtailed electricity is produced using fossil fuels. Fleets won't have to watch OPEC or the global oil markets to gauge next quarter's fuel costs. They can lock in local electricity rates and produce hydrogen on-site or nearby.

Fleet managers are inherently pragmatic. They want solutions that work **now**, not in 10 years. Hydrogen delivers lower, more predictable fuel costs, reduced maintenance, fast refueling, and zero emissions. Each fleet that transitions strengthens the overall ecosystem, driving down costs and spurring more infrastructure. It's a **virtuous cycle** that benefits everyone, from business owners and drivers to local communities and the environment.

As we head into Chapter 9, "Grid Stabilization and Energy Security," we'll explore how fleets of hydrogen vehicles can help **balance and stabilize the electrical grid**. Picture a future where trucks not only consume clean energy, but also give back to the grid when needed. The technology to do this is already in pilot stages across the country.

Conclusion for Chapter 8

Converting America's fleets to hydrogen isn't a distant dream; it's an immediately actionable opportunity. By starting with trucks, the largest users of diesel, we address a massive source of emissions while creating a practical business case that saves money and streamlines operations. Fleets can refuel quickly, carry full payloads, and turn otherwise wasted electricity into a clean, high-value fuel. Best of all, each success story paves the way for broader adoption, helping us strengthen our grid, our economy, and our energy independence. The transition is happening now. Those who move first will reap the greatest rewards.

Chapter 9:

Grid Stabilization and Energy Security: The Foundation of America's Energy Future

On August 14, 2003, at precisely 4:10 PM EST, more than 50 million Americans and Canadians found themselves suddenly plunged into darkness. The Northeast blackout, which began with a seemingly harmless software bug in Ohio, escalated into the largest power outage in North American history. It shut down 265 power plants in just seven minutes. Water systems failed, cell networks collapsed, and 11 people lost their lives. The total economic impact? $6 billion.[40]

This catastrophic event exposed a fundamental weakness in our nation's power grid—its fragility when confronted with sudden fluctuations in power supply and demand. Fast forward twenty years, and our ongoing transition to renewable energy has heightened these fluctuations even more. Grid operators walk a tightrope each day, trying to balance the intermittent nature of wind and solar power with society's constant appetite for electricity.

That very instability, however, could become our greatest asset—fueling America's path to genuine energy independence. Consider the Texas winter storm in 2021. Millions lost power as frozen wind turbines and natural gas lines simultaneously failed. Now imagine a different world: massive hydrogen storage facilities, brimming with excess wind energy from the previous summer, stood ready to power not just emergency generators but entire cities through the crisis. Far from science fiction, this scenario is feasible today with existing technology.[41]

Right now, our electric grid looks like a giant game of Jenga. Operators carefully add and remove power sources, striving for perfect balance, while one wrong move can topple everything. This delicate balancing act costs utilities billions of dollars in frequency regulation. There is a constant, split-second struggle to match demand. Grid stabilization, though, goes far beyond keeping the lights on. It's also about national security, economic prosperity, and global competitiveness. When major technology firms pick locations for their data centers—facilities that can guzzle as much electricity as small cities—the first question they ask is always about power reliability. A single minute of downtime can mean millions in losses.

What's the solution? It's not simply adding more plants or stringing up more transmission lines. Instead, we need to rethink how we store and manage energy. Hydrogen storage technology can create a robust, flexible grid capable of absorbing and releasing energy exactly when needed—be that in five minutes or five months. In other words, hydrogen can turn our vulnerable, inefficient system into the backbone of American energy independence.

The Dance of Electrons: Bringing Balance to America's Power Grid

Visualize stepping into the control room at the California Independent System Operator (CAISO) on a scorching summer afternoon. Towering screens display real-time data from thousands of power sources across the state. A supervisor spots something ominous: a massive cloud bank rolling over the Mojave Desert is about to slice solar production by 70% at one of the world's largest solar installations. Meanwhile, millions of Californians are returning home, cranking up their air conditioners, and creating the dreaded "duck curve" of surging demand.[42]

In the past, this would trigger emergency measures: firing up costly, polluting peaker plants, begging neighboring states for extra power at premium prices, or even resorting to rolling blackouts. However, in the near future, we can envision the supervisor simply watching as automated systems draw from a network of hydrogen storage facilities sprinkled across the state. The transition is so seamless that Californians go about their evening routines unaware of the behind-the-scenes choreography keeping the lights on.

This is about more than preventing blackouts. Traditional power plants ramp up and down like a car constantly accelerating and braking in heavy traffic, wasting fuel and damaging equipment. This strain costs utilities billions each year in maintenance and reduced efficiency. It's akin to driving your car by flooring the gas, and then slamming on the brakes, over and over.

There's a deeper security angle here, too. The Government Accountability Office identified many successful cyberattacks on America's power infrastructure in 2021 alone.[43] Each attack highlighted a vulnerability: our centralized, just-in-time delivery system. A single well-placed strike can trigger failures across entire regions. Distributing hydrogen storage facilities, however, adds multiple layers of redundancy. Instead of relying on long-distance transmission lines that could be disrupted by anything from hackers to curious squirrels (which cause hundreds of outages each year), communities would maintain their own power reserves.

Ultimately, hydrogen offers more than just light in a storm—its strategic placement in rural communities can foster true energy independence. These regions, often perched at the end of long transmission lines, can store excess wind and solar power during peak production and tap into it during shortages or emergencies. This new approach is an economic revolution waiting to happen. The same hydrogen that stabilizes our grid can fuel clean industries—from steel production to heavy-duty transportation—providing jobs, growth, and greater energy security.

Harnessing Chaos: The Symphony of Smart Energy Management

Picture a vast wind farm in Iowa, the blades slicing through the quiet midnight air. It's 2:00 AM, and these turbines generate enough electricity to power three million homes. The trouble is that only one million homes need power at that time of night. In our current system, operators must either curtail wind production—throwing away clean energy—or sell it at negative prices, paying other utilities to take it.[44]

Now, envision a different reality: the same wind farm paired with a sophisticated hydrogen production facility, effectively acting as a giant battery for America's heartland. Every watt of surplus electricity is converted to hydrogen, stored, and ready to power anything from local factories to long-haul trucks. This is energy storage on a grand scale, turning what was once wasted into pure opportunity.

That payoff goes far beyond economics. Data centers in Silicon Valley, for example, currently rely on massive battery arrays and diesel generators to ward off microsecond power fluctuations that could crash their servers. Hydrogen-based systems could replace these costly backups, delivering both primary and emergency power without polluting the air.

The Port of Los Angeles provides another prime example. Huge swings in energy demand occur as container ships connect or disconnect from shore power, putting a strain on the local grid. A hydrogen-based power management system could smooth these spikes while fueling the port's zero-emission vehicles and equipment. Even more exciting, hydrogen systems excel at frequency regulation—the rapid-fire adjustments that keep the grid humming at precisely 60 hertz. Rather than natural gas plants revving up and down—wasting fuel and incurring wear—hydrogen-based systems can respond almost instantly, with no emissions and no mechanical tear.

Imagine it like a symphony. In a traditional grid, each musician struggles to stay in sync on their own. With hydrogen, you gain a master conductor, orchestrating every note perfectly; this is more than a technical fix: it's a complete reimagining of how we distribute energy. Each hydrogen facility becomes a node in a massive, intelligent network that absorbs or releases power as needed, drastically simplifying what has been a precarious balancing act.

The Digital Fortress: Securing America's Energy Future Through Grid Intelligence

Deep in the Rocky Mountains sits a seemingly ordinary warehouse that might just be the future of American energy security. Inside, rows of electrolyzer stacks quietly convert excess wind energy into hydrogen. Yet, the real magic is the artificial intelligence orchestrating every move. This AI system crunches weather data, demand forecasts, and grid conditions across six states, adjusting production in real time to keep the regional grid rock solid.

Think of it as a sort of air traffic control but for electricity. When a sudden blizzard disrupts Wyoming wind farms, stored hydrogen flows through fuel cells to compensate. If Colorado's solar arrays spike under unexpected sunshine, surplus power is funneled into hydrogen production, avoiding dangerous overloads. The operation is accurate to the millisecond, maintaining stable voltage and frequency over thousands of miles of power lines.

The national security implications are massive. The Department of Defense cites grid vulnerability as a top threat. One well-executed cyberattack could knock out large swaths of our energy infrastructure. But a decentralized network of hydrogen storage facilities—each capable of running independently—creates a system that's incredibly tough to take down entirely.

On the economic front, power quality issues cost American businesses a whopping $150 billion every year. According to Fastech, a hydrogen-based grid can help stabilize the grid and could slash losses drastically.[45] That's a big boost to manufacturers whose bottom line hinges on reliable, clean power.

This approach also democratizes energy storage. Small communities can own hydrogen systems, storing extra renewable energy and using it during outages. For example, a rural hospital in Montana integrated an electrolyzer with its existing solar array, achieving near-complete self-sufficiency. That same hydrogen also fuels the hospital's fleet of delivery vans.[46]

As we retire traditional power plants, hydrogen systems can provide that critical "grid inertia" once offered by the heavy spinning turbines of coal and gas plants. Unlike mechanical systems, though, hydrogen can respond in an instant, offering stability that's faster, cleaner, and more reliable. The technology is here. The math adds up. Now, it's about whether we have the vision to scale it nationwide.

The Grid of Tomorrow: From Vulnerability to Victory

As we look across America, it's clear we're at a pivotal point in energy history. The choices we make about our grid—from how we store energy to how we protect it—will shape our economy, our security, and our environment for generations. Already, research centers in the Nevada desert are testing a concept they've nicknamed the Infinity Grid: a lightning-fast system that merges AI-driven controls, hydrogen storage, and renewables in ways once considered impossible.

At the Nevada Desert Research Center, this Infinity Grid can flick from solar power to stored hydrogen in under 50 milliseconds—quicker than a blink. It can also operate in what's known as "dark start" mode, using hydrogen alone to restart a completely de-energized grid sector without external power. That's not just an engineering triumph, it's a template for energy sovereignty. Every hydrogen storage facility is like an energy fortress—each electrolyzer a building block of independence. At scale, these systems won't just stabilize our grid; they'll reduce reliance on foreign energy and create a sustainable cycle of domestic growth.

The numbers are staggering. The Department of Energy estimates American businesses suffer $150 billion in annual losses from power quality issues alone. Hydrogen storage could cut those losses by 90%, and create new revenue streams from clean fuel production and frequency regulation services. It's like turning each utility into a bank for energy, storing surplus power and dispensing it where and when it's needed most.

Meanwhile, the beauty of hydrogen-based grid stabilization is that it works everywhere. A small town can achieve energy independence with a modest system; factories get the high-quality power they need; hospitals enjoy uninterrupted service; large-scale infrastructure can scale up seamlessly, weaving a patchwork of resilient energy hubs across the nation.

It won't happen overnight. Our current grid took decades to build, and we'll have to navigate regulatory hurdles, develop skilled workforces, and secure solid financing models. But the central question remains: will we continue patching up an outdated framework or boldly construct a new one?

As we move on to Chapter 10, "Beyond Transportation," we'll see that hydrogen's potential doesn't end with stabilizing the grid. The very hydrogen that keeps our lights on can power our industries, heat our homes, and fuel our vehicles. It can turn what used to be waste into a transformative, clean-energy opportunity.

Conclusion for Chapter 9

America's grid is at a crossroads. Our aging infrastructure is increasingly strained by severe weather events, cyber threats, and the growing demands of a modern, digital society. Yet, out of these challenges emerges an opportunity. By leveraging hydrogen storage and advanced, AI-driven energy management, we can build a power system that's stable, secure, and clean.

Throughout this chapter, we've seen hydrogen-based solutions at every level—from rural hospitals sustaining power during emergencies to entire towns that run off stored energy for days at a time. We've glimpsed the vast potential of AI-guided "energy traffic control" and the promise of the Infinity Grid to eliminate downtime entirely. Most importantly, we've discovered how taking a fresh look at our grid—viewing it not just as a delivery mechanism but as a dynamic, flexible network—frees us from old vulnerabilities.

The path forward isn't a matter of if, but when. The technology exists. The economics make sense. The momentum is building. As we forge ahead, hydrogen offers more than just an energy fix—it offers a chance to redefine America's power landscape for decades to come, ensuring a resilient, secure, and prosperous future for all.

Chapter 10:

Beyond Transportation—Hydrogen's Unlimited Potential

When I first encountered hydrogen in my eighth-grade science class, it felt like nothing more than a simple experiment—splitting water into hydrogen and oxygen through electrolysis. We all did it. None of us died. None of our schools blew up. It was just a straightforward demonstration involving the universe's most abundant element.

What I didn't appreciate at the time—although it's become crystal clear after 35 years of studying this technology—is that hydrogen goes far beyond a cool science project or even just a next-generation transportation fuel. It has the potential to secure America's energy independence across every sector of our economy.

In the previous chapter, we explored how hydrogen could revolutionize our electrical grid—eliminating waste, tackling negative pricing, and delivering genuine energy security. That was just scratching the surface. The true power of hydrogen lies in its extraordinary versatility: it can serve multiple purposes simultaneously, in ways that batteries or other storage systems cannot match.

Let's start with a concrete example. Take a poultry processing plant. Most of us would look at it and see a single operation. I see five or six different hydrogen applications under one roof: powering the facility's electricity, heating water for sanitation, fueling forklifts to move products, heating the building, and even powering distribution trucks. No other energy carrier can serve all these functions with zero emissions, where the only byproduct is water vapor.

This flexibility is why hydrogen is so revolutionary. While everyone else tries to shoehorn batteries into jobs they're not suited for, we have an opportunity to deploy hydrogen as a complete energy solution, powering everything from steel mills to farming operations, all with existing technology. The core principles we learned in eighth grade have been refined over 175 years; what's been missing is the vision to assemble all the pieces.[47]

In this chapter, we'll explore how hydrogen can transform some of America's most essential industries—from steel production to agriculture to manufacturing. We'll examine real-world applications that can be deployed today using existing infrastructure. Ultimately, we'll see how these facets unite into a single energy ecosystem that keeps American dollars on American soil, cleans up our environment, and strengthens our economy.

The path forward isn't about swapping out one form of energy for another. It's about creating an integrated system that meets all our energy demands while boosting American competitiveness and national security. That's the promise of hydrogen—and that's what we're about to dive into.

The Heart of American Industry: Steel Production and Hydrogen's Role

Few things are more fundamental to a nation's manufacturing independence than steel. No advanced society can remain sovereign without the ability to produce its own steel. Today, however, environmental concerns and industrial needs often collide, leaving the steel industry at a crossroads. Hydrogen offers a way out of this impasse, satisfying both environmental requirements and production imperatives.

I'm not suggesting we eliminate all oil or petrochemicals—those products have their rightful place in manufacturing everything from medical devices to crucial materials. What I'm proposing is a strategic shift in how we power core industries like steel. Traditional methods rely on coal and coke to generate the enormous heat required in blast furnaces, leading to heavy emissions and making us dependent on foreign energy sources. By switching to hydrogen, we maintain the high temperatures but cut emissions dramatically, releasing only water vapor.

Here's where it gets interesting. We can produce the needed hydrogen using the same "curtailed" electricity (excess power from the grid, both renewable and not) that utilities are paying people to take. Instead of throwing money at foreign oil suppliers or discarding unused energy, we can deploy homegrown resources to strengthen our industrial base.

Regions where steel facilities and robust renewable resources coexist—like Pennsylvania and much of the Midwest—are particularly well-positioned. Excess grid power of all types can feed hydrogen production, which in turn fuels steel-making. It's a closed-loop system that fortifies our manufacturing backbone, keeps energy dollars local, and diminishes our reliance on outside resources.

This shift isn't hypothetical. Hydrogen-based steel production is already rolling out in Europe. America could leapfrog everyone else because we have one crucial edge: vast amounts of energy currently going to waste. Rather than overhauling everything, we can begin by using our existing energy more intelligently.

It's not just about the environment either. It's about safeguarding American industries, creating jobs, and preserving the capabilities that protect our national independence. When I say "energy independence," I'm talking about far more than what fuels your car. It includes having the means to power our most vital industries without leaning on foreign suppliers.

By leveraging hydrogen in steel production, we unify environmental stewardship with bottom-line profitability. It's not a competition between the economy and the environment—innovative American engineering can serve both simultaneously.

Agricultural Revolution: From Waste to Wealth

Nowhere is hydrogen's transformative power more obvious than in the agricultural sector. Agriculture ranks among our nation's largest energy consumers—fueling farm equipment, producing fertilizers, and processing and transporting food. It also generates huge amounts of waste that could be converted into clean energy, making hydrogen a game-changer.

Consider the operations in California's Central Valley. Massive dairy farms generate tons of cow waste that can be used to create biogas. In Merced County, one of the largest methane digesters was developed specifically to capture cow manure biogas. They line a giant pit, cover it, and ferment the manure to produce methane, which powers a gas turbine, generating electricity and producing heat for steam to clean the facility. Joseph Gallo Farms pioneered this system two decades ago, powering plant operations and cheese production all in one integrated loop.[48]

Hydrogen brings this concept to a new level. Biogas can feed directly into hydrogen production, turning farms into self-sustaining energy hubs. Hydrogen can then power tractors and trucks, heat buildings, or even be sold off-site as a revenue source—all from what used to be waste.

Every large farm could follow Gallo's lead, generating clean hydrogen from biomass byproducts. This fuels their equipment, provides hot water, and meets their transportation needs. Surplus hydrogen can be sold, creating a brand-new stream of income. It's a virtuous cycle: agriculture produces waste, which creates energy, which powers more agricultural production—all with reduced emissions and local economic benefits.[49]

This is not a theory. It's been proven on a small scope, waiting to be scaled up. When we weave these agricultural energy hubs into the broader hydrogen economy—connecting them to steel plants, cement plants, transportation fleets, and even our national grid—we see how hydrogen unifies disparate industries into a cohesive, emission-free system.

Agriculture is ripe for this shift because it needs cleaner energy and has the resources to produce it. It's a prime example of solving multiple challenges simultaneously while driving American independence and revitalizing rural communities.

Industrial Heat: The Missing Link in Clean Energy

A commonly overlooked aspect of our energy transition is high-grade industrial heat. While everyone zeroes in on electricity and transportation, many manufacturing processes demand extreme temperatures that battery technology or basic renewables can't easily provide. Hydrogen fills this gap beautifully, becoming the final piece of a comprehensive clean-energy puzzle.

Take cement production. It's among the most energy-intensive processes on the planet. It relies on fossil fuels to hit the extreme temperatures needed for kiln operations. As a result, it's also one of the largest industrial sources of greenhouse gas emissions. Replace coal or natural gas with hydrogen, and you achieve the same heat output with no carbon emissions.

Switching to hydrogen for industrial heat extends beyond climate benefits. The same hydrogen that fires a cement kiln can also run on-site vehicles, generate electricity, or heat office buildings within the facility. Rather than juggling multiple energy systems—diesel, electricity, natural gas—you can run a single hydrogen-based network. It streamlines operations, cuts maintenance costs, and creates economies of scale.

With much of America's industrial infrastructure aging out, we're at a juncture to make bold changes. As old fossil fuel systems require upgrades, we can invest in hydrogen-based replacements that offer more flexibility and reduced emissions. The economic argument strengthens when these facilities double as energy hubs, producing or storing hydrogen to share with local fleets or providing backup power during outages.

Hydrogen's unique advantage is its storability. Electricity must be used immediately or the battery stored at high costs; instead, hydrogen can be produced whenever surplus power is available and stockpiled indefinitely. That means factories can tap cheap or curtailed energy, convert it to hydrogen, and draw on it for industrial heat whenever they need it. This synergy fosters partnerships between utilities (who gain a steady buyer for excess energy) and industries (which gain a clean, reliable heat source).

Export Opportunities: America's Green Energy Leadership stopped

Our nation faces a golden opportunity to not only achieve energy independence but to become a net exporter of clean energy. Thanks to abundant renewable capacity, manufacturing prowess, and proven technologies, we can lead the global hydrogen revolution—shifting from an importer of oil to an exporter of green solutions.

A prime example of this potential is ammonia. Already a vital agricultural fertilizer, ammonia also acts as an excellent hydrogen carrier that can be transported using existing infrastructure. By utilizing our surplus wind and solar energy to produce hydrogen, then converting it to ammonia, we gain a valuable, exportable commodity. It's a win-win: energy can be stored and shipped to places that might lack similar renewable resources.

However, the priority remains domestic security. Before exporting, we should first ensure that America's needs are met: powering truck fleets, industrial processes, and our electricity grid. Once those bases are covered, we can share our surplus energy solutions with the world.

Another exciting part is how naturally this progression unfolds. As we master hydrogen production, storage, and usage here at home, we build expertise that other countries will pay for—both in the form of clean fuel and the know-how to implement it. Our agricultural states in the Great Plains—already curtailing wind energy—could transform that excess power into hydrogen or ammonia for global markets, turning wasted energy into thriving new export industries.

Worldwide, countries are hungry for clean energy, and the United States holds a unique combination of resources and technical expertise. By moving swiftly, we can establish ourselves as the leading innovator in the hydrogen sphere, exporting not just energy but the entire blueprint for a functioning hydrogen economy.

The Future Is Here: From Theory to Implementation

Three decades ago, people called me a dreamer for saying hydrogen could reshape the energy landscape. They said it was too expensive, too risky, too far-fetched. Yet, every single one of those concerns has crumbled under the weight of real-world progress.

In this chapter, we've seen how hydrogen can overhaul steel production, revolutionize agriculture, provide high-grade industrial heat, and even open export opportunities. The magic of hydrogen isn't in doing just one of these things; it's that it can accomplish all of them at once, forming a unified energy ecosystem.

Picture a steel plant in Pennsylvania running on hydrogen generated from wind farms in the region. Oxygen byproduct from electrolysis is piped to medical facilities. Heat from fuel cells helps maintain production temperatures. Extra hydrogen powers the on-site vehicle fleet. And, over in California, a dairy operation transforms cow manure into biogas that's converted into hydrogen, powering everything from farm equipment to distribution trucks. Any surplus enters a local hydrogen network, fueling trucks or industrial users nearby.

This is not a far-future fantasy. Every element already exists. We're just missing the widespread determination to implement it. The payoff extends well beyond decarbonization. Every dollar spent on domestic energy is a dollar that stays in our communities, creating jobs, strengthening local economies, and cutting dependence on foreign energy.

This is why I've invested my life into promoting hydrogen. It's not just about a cleaner planet. It's about a wealthier, more self-reliant America. Why throw away energy or rely on imports when we can power ourselves at home? Every day we stall is another day we send energy dollars overseas and squander resources that could be fueling American prosperity.

We learned in eighth-grade science that the simplest solutions can be the most powerful. We don't need outlandish breakthroughs—just the will to use what we already have more wisely. Hydrogen isn't some distant technology. It's here, it works, and it's ready to propel us into a new era of American energy independence.

Conclusion: The Hydrogen Path Forward

Hydrogen's promise goes far beyond any single application. Throughout this chapter, we saw how it can meet diverse energy demands across steel production, agriculture, industrial heating, and even global exports. What ties all of these opportunities together is hydrogen's unmatched versatility and storability. By harnessing excess renewable power—and even agricultural waste—we create a resilient, closed-loop energy network that boosts American industry, safeguards our environment, and keeps dollars circulating in our communities.

The core takeaway is simple: hydrogen is not theoretical. It's real, it's proven, and it's ready for deployment. Whether we're talking about a dairy farm in California, a steel mill in Pennsylvania, or an export hub in the Midwest, the foundational components already exist. Moving forward requires vision, collaboration, and the courage to invest in infrastructure that will pay dividends for generations. If we seize this opportunity, we'll make good on the promise of true energy independence—transforming not just how we power our cars, but how we power our entire nation.

Chapter 11:

The 12-Month Plan: Turning Vision into Reality

Back in 1973, America was brought to its knees by an oil embargo that sent gas prices skyrocketing overnight, from around 25 cents to nearly $2 per gallon in just weeks. This crisis led to the creation of the Department of Energy, established with the promise that America would never again be so vulnerable to foreign energy manipulation. Yet, fifty years later, we're still sending billions of dollars overseas for oil, still at risk to foreign markets, and still wasting massive amounts of domestic energy that could be powering our economy.

I've spent decades watching history repeat itself. In the previous chapters, we explored the tremendous potential of hydrogen across multiple sectors of our economy—from steel production to agriculture, from industrial processes to export opportunities. But potential means nothing without action. We can't afford to spend another fifty years talking about energy independence while sending our wealth overseas.

That's why I believe we need a focused, twelve-month plan to begin this transition. Not a fifty-year roadmap. Not a theoretical framework. A practical, implementable plan that starts with the resources and technology we already have. The utility companies are producing excess energy. The truck manufacturers know how to build hydrogen-powered vehicles. Industrial users need cleaner energy solutions. We don't need to wait for futuristic technology or massive infrastructure buildouts. We need to connect these existing pieces into a coherent system now.

When I look at Pacific Gas & Electric with its 14,000 medium and heavy-duty trucks, I see an opportunity to begin this transition immediately. They're currently paying to curtail excess energy while also paying for diesel fuel. That makes no economic sense. With the right implementation plan, they could be using their own wasted energy to power their vehicles within months, not years.

In this chapter, we'll lay out a phase-by-phase, twelve-month plan for implementing hydrogen solutions—one that's based on existing technology and real-world opportunities. Think of it as a practical roadmap that starts with a few strategic projects and scales up, connecting each success story into a comprehensive hydrogen economy. The time for pilot projects and endless feasibility studies is over. We already have what we need to act.

Phase 1 (Months 1–3): Strategic Fleet Conversion

The first phase is all about what I call "matched-pair implementation": identifying utility companies that have both significant energy curtailment and large vehicle fleets suitable for hydrogen conversion. Rather than building hydrogen infrastructure and hoping customers appear, we match existing supply with guaranteed demand.

1. **Identify Key Utilities:** Focus on utilities with notable curtailment—where they're forced to discard or pay to move excess power—and large internal fleets burning expensive diesel.
2. **Calculate Supply & Demand:** Work out exactly how many megawatt-hours are being curtailed and how much diesel is being purchased. For context, 1 MWh can produce about 20 kilograms of hydrogen—enough to power a heavy-duty truck for around 1,400 miles.
3. **Launch Small-Scale Pilot Sites:** Convert a manageable subset of each fleet operating from a central location. This lets you perfect systems on a smaller scale, measure real-world performance, and generate data that proves the concept's feasibility.

Every kilogram of hydrogen produced from curtailed energy turns waste into value. The financial upside creates immediate incentives for the utilities and fleet operators involved. By the end of this phase, we aim to have at least one or two successful "matched-pair" conversions demonstrating real economic and environmental benefits.

Phase 2 (Months 4–6): Infrastructure Development

With initial conversions underway, the second phase focuses on building out the critical hydrogen infrastructure—but in a targeted, demand-driven way rather than a speculative buildout. The idea is to install production and fueling capacity where we already know it will be used.

1. **Utility Energy Capture Points:** Establish hydrogen production hubs directly at the sites where curtailment is highest, minimizing transmission losses.
2. **Fleet Service Centers:** Upgrade existing maintenance and fueling facilities to handle hydrogen. Drivers and mechanics can adapt to hydrogen more comfortably if they're at the same depot they've always used.
3. **Industrial Anchor Points:** Place production facilities near large industrial users—steel plants, food processors, or manufacturers—that can benefit immediately from cleaner energy or high-temperature hydrogen processes.

This approach sets up a network of fully utilized infrastructure from day one. It's also more attractive to investors because each facility has a guaranteed user base, like fleet operators and industrial plants, as well as a clear revenue model. By the end of month six, we aim to have multiple hydrogen "nodes" across different regions, each serving a specific, immediate need and ready to scale further.

Phase 3 (Months 7–9): Grid Integration & Stabilization

With initial production facilities in place, we can unlock hydrogen's broader potential as a grid stabilization tool. This goes beyond transportation fuel: hydrogen becomes the buffer that absorbs excess electricity and evens out supply-demand imbalances.

1. **Responsive Hydrogen Production:** Implement control systems that automatically increase or decrease hydrogen production based on grid conditions. If there's a spike in wind or solar output, direct it to hydrogen generation instead of curtailment.

2. **Dynamic Storage Management:** Store hydrogen in tanks or underground caverns. Then, use it when fleets need to fuel up or when the grid could benefit from fuel-cell power during peak demand.
3. **Cross-Facility Coordination:** Link hydrogen production sites so that if one facility is nearing storage limits, excess energy can be routed to a site that still has capacity. This unified network strengthens overall grid reliability.

By the end of month nine, every hydrogen facility should be a strategic asset; not just producing fuel but also providing valuable grid services. This integrated model allows utilities to monetize what was previously wasted, turning curtailed electricity into a lucrative revenue stream.

Phase 4 (Months 10–12): Industrial Adoption & Ecosystems

Once fleets have converted and the hydrogen infrastructure is functioning, the final phase focuses on industrial applications. This is where hydrogen truly outperforms other clean-energy options, as many industries need high-grade heat or chemical feedstocks that batteries can't provide.

1. **Identify High-Energy Industries:** Steel mills, cement plants, food processing facilities—any large operation that requires consistent power, heat, or process energy.
2. **Co-Locate and Integrate:** Position hydrogen production near these industrial plants to minimize transport costs and maximize efficiency. The facility that fuels trucks can also supply hydrogen for furnaces or chemical processes.
3. **"Hub and Spoke" Model:** Each industrial center becomes a hydrogen "hub." Surrounding businesses—distribution centers, farms, smaller manufacturers—can connect as "spokes," tapping into the hub's capacity.

By the end of the twelfth month, we want several industrial sites fully or partially running on hydrogen, reinforcing that this isn't just about vehicles. It's about comprehensive energy ecosystems.

Financing the Future

For any energy project, the question of "Who pays for it?" looms large. Hydrogen's versatility actually creates financial advantages if we capture **all** its value streams: curtailment avoidance, grid services, stable fuel pricing, and emissions reductions.

- **Energy Service Agreements:** Utilities can monetize hydrogen production the same way they monetize electricity: stable revenue tied to actual grid and fleet needs.
- **Fleet Conversion Leases:** Truck operators can lease hydrogen vehicles, paying off the capital costs through fuel savings over time.
- **Industrial Partnerships:** Large energy users can co-invest in hydrogen facilities that also provide them with a more secure and cheaper energy supply.

By properly accounting for saved curtailment costs, improved grid stability, and reduced dependence on volatile fossil-fuel markets, the business case for hydrogen often stands on its own. These aren't pie-in-the-sky, subsidy-dependent proposals. They're viable, bankable projects once the calculation includes every benefit.

Creating the New Energy Economy: Jobs and Communities

A thriving hydrogen economy isn't just about technology or economics; it's about people. We'll need new technicians, mechanics, and engineers. However, many existing skill sets can transition easily to hydrogen. A diesel mechanic already understands the fundamentals of vehicle repair. From there, learning to maintain hydrogen drivetrains is a manageable step. Also, an electrician can adapt from conventional power systems to hydrogen production and fuel cells with targeted training.

- **Local Job Creation:** Each 20 MW hydrogen facility creates permanent operations, maintenance, and administrative positions.
- **Workforce Development:** Community colleges and trade schools can offer hydrogen certification programs, ensuring a steady

pipeline of qualified workers.

- **Resilience and Community Benefits:** By producing and storing fuel locally, communities gain backup power options for emergencies, reduce pollution, and keep energy dollars circulating in the local economy.

Measuring Success: Beyond the Bottom Line

To track whether these projects deliver on their promises, we need a three-pronged measurement framework:

1. **Economic:** Look beyond direct hydrogen revenue to include avoided curtailment costs, reduced diesel spending, and stable fuel pricing.
2. **Operational:** Measure energy capture efficiency (the percentage of curtailed power successfully turned into hydrogen), plus vehicle performance and fueling reliability.
3. **Strategic:** Evaluate foreign oil imports replaced, resilience during grid outages, new export possibilities, and long-term local economic growth.

By the end of month eleven, each site should have baseline metrics in place. By month twelve, the data is compiled, analyzed, and shared, forming a powerful evidence base to fuel further expansion.

Beyond Year One: Scaling the Hydrogen Revolution

The first twelve months are about proof of concept—building tangible examples in select regions. Once these sites show hydrogen's economic, operational, and strategic value, adoption will accelerate naturally:

- **Geographic Expansion:** Convert isolated clusters into full-scale hydrogen corridors connecting major interstate routes and industrial zones.
- **Application Diversity:** Move beyond fleets and industrial processes to heating, refrigeration, and eventually large-scale export.
- **Network Integration:** Link multiple sites so they can balance each

other's production and storage, creating a national hydrogen ecosystem.

With each successful demonstration, more companies and communities jump on board. It's a ripple effect. Once a waste management company saves money by running hydrogen trucks, competitors quickly follow. Once a utility profits by turning curtailed wind into fuel, others replicate the model.

Your Role in America's Energy Future

Whether you're a utility executive, truck operator, industrial manager, investor, policymaker, or an interested citizen, you have a role to play. The technology is here. The economics make sense. The need for reliable, domestic energy has never been more urgent. Each of us can do something:

- **Utilities:** Monetize your curtailed energy by producing hydrogen instead of paying others to take your excess.
- **Fleet Managers:** Stabilize your fuel costs and reduce maintenance headaches by switching to hydrogen vehicles.
- **Industrial Operators:** Integrate hydrogen to power high-heat processes and insulate yourselves from volatile fossil-fuel prices.
- **Communities & Policymakers:** Support zoning, permitting, training, and incentive structures that enable hydrogen projects to launch and thrive.

Energy transitions don't happen to us. We make them happen. This moment is an opportunity to reshape our energy landscape for the better, making it cleaner, more stable, and undeniably American.

Conclusion: A New Independence Day

America's energy history has been marked by paradox—vast domestic resources on one hand, heavy foreign fuel dependence on the other. The plan described here is about closing that gap by using what we already have: curtailed power, proven electrolyzer and fuel-cell technology, and a national appetite for energy independence.

Over the next twelve months, we can begin building hydrogen's foundation. We start small, converting a few fleets and facilities. We prove the concept, scale up, link different regions, and integrate industries. Along the way, we create jobs, strengthen communities, and keep energy dollars circulating domestically.

What happens after that is up to us. If we seize this opportunity, we can rewrite America's energy story. One where no foreign oil sits on U.S. soil. Because we have more than enough domestic capacity to meet our needs. It won't take half a century or revolutionary breakthroughs. It'll take leadership, cooperation, and decisive action.

That transformation can start now. This is our new Independence Day—the moment we stop talking about **energy dominance** and start creating it.

Green Hydrogen, Renewable Energy & Electricity Glossary

A

- **Alternating Current (AC)** – An electric current that periodically reverses direction, used in most electrical grids.
- **Amperes (Amps, A)** – A unit of electric current that measures the flow of electric charge.
- **Ancillary Services** – Support services that help maintain the reliability of the electricity grid, such as frequency regulation and spinning reserves.
- **Anode** – The electrode where oxidation occurs in an electrochemical reaction, such as in electrolysis or batteries.
- **Availability Factor** – The percentage of time that a power generation facility is available to produce electricity.

B

- **Base Load** – The minimum level of electricity demand that must be met at all times.
- **Battery Energy Storage System (BESS)** – A system used to store excess electricity for later use, commonly paired with renewable energy.
- **Blackout** – A total loss of electricity supply in a grid or region.
- **Biomass Energy** – Renewable energy derived from organic materials like wood, agricultural residues, and waste.

C

- **Capacity Factor** – The ratio of actual energy generated by a power plant to its maximum possible output over a specific period.
- **Carbon Capture and Storage (CCS)** – Technology used to capture and store CO_2 emissions from industrial sources.
- **Circuit Breaker** – A safety device that interrupts electrical flow when a fault is detected.
- **Combined Cycle Power Plant (CCPP)** – A power plant that uses

both gas and steam turbines to generate electricity more efficiently.

- **Current (I)** – The flow of electric charge, measured in amperes (A).

D

- **DC (Direct Current)** – Electric current that flows in one direction, commonly used in batteries and solar panels.
- **Demand Response** – A strategy where electricity consumers adjust usage in response to grid signals, improving efficiency.
- **Dispatchable Energy** – Power sources that can be turned on or off to meet demand fluctuations, like natural gas or hydroelectric plants.
- **Distributed Generation** – Small-scale electricity generation close to the point of consumption, often involving renewables.

E

- **Electrolysis** – The process of using electricity to split water (H_2O) into hydrogen (H_2) and oxygen (O_2).
- **Energy Efficiency** – The ratio of useful energy output to energy input in a system, expressed as a percentage.
- **Energy Density** – The amount of energy stored per unit of volume or mass, relevant for fuels and batteries.
- **Energy Mix** – The combination of different energy sources (e.g., fossil fuels, nuclear, renewables) used to generate electricity in a grid.
- **Exajoule (EJ)** – A unit of energy equal to one quintillion (10^{18}) joules, used to measure global energy consumption.

F

- **Feed-in Tariff (FiT)** – A policy that guarantees payments to renewable energy producers for the electricity they generate.
- **Frequency (Hz)** – The rate at which an alternating current (AC) oscillates per second, measured in hertz (Hz). The standard frequency is **50 Hz or 60 Hz,** depending on the country.

- **Fuel Cell** – A device that generates electricity through an electrochemical reaction between hydrogen and oxygen.

G

- **Gigawatt (GW)** – A unit of power equal to **1 billion watts (10^9 W)**, used to measure large-scale power plants.
- **Grid Parity** – The point at which renewable energy costs the same or less than fossil fuel-based electricity.
- **Grid Resilience** – The ability of an electricity grid to withstand and recover from disruptions, such as extreme weather events.

H

- **Hydropower** – Electricity generated from flowing or falling water, commonly using dams or river-based systems.
- **High Voltage (HV)** – Electrical transmission at high voltages (typically above **69 kV**) to reduce energy loss over long distances.

I

- **Installed Capacity** – The total maximum output a power plant or energy system can produce.
- **Interconnection** – The physical and electrical linking of different power grids for improved stability and energy exchange.
- **Intermittency** – The variability of renewable energy sources like solar and wind, which do not generate power continuously.

J

- **Joule (J)** – A unit of energy, where **1 watt-second = 1 joule**.

K

- **Kilowatt (kW)** – A unit of power equal to **1,000 watts**.
- **Kilowatt-hour (kWh)** – A unit of energy equal to one kilowatt of power used over one hour.

L

- **Levelized Cost of Energy (LCOE)** – A measure of the average total cost to build and operate a power plant per unit of electricity generated.

- **Load Shedding** – The deliberate shutdown of power in parts of a grid to prevent system overload and blackouts.
- **Low-Carbon Energy** – Energy sources that produce minimal greenhouse gas emissions, such as nuclear, hydro, and renewables.

M

- **Megawatt (MW)** – A unit of power equal to **1 million watts (10^6 W)**.
- **Megawatt-hour (MWh)** – A unit of energy equivalent to consuming **1 MW of power for one hour**.
- **Microgrid** – A localized power grid that can operate independently or in conjunction with the main grid.
- **Molten Salt Storage** – A method of storing thermal energy for later use, commonly used in **concentrated solar power (CSP)** plants.

N

- **Net Metering** – A system where customers with renewable energy systems (e.g., solar panels) can send excess electricity to the grid in exchange for credits.
- **Nuclear Energy** – Energy produced through nuclear fission, where atoms are split to release energy.

O

- **Off-grid** – A system that generates and stores its own electricity without being connected to the main grid.

P

- **Peak Load** – The highest level of electricity demand in a given period.
- **Photovoltaic (PV) Solar Energy** – Electricity generated by converting sunlight directly into electricity using solar panels.
- **Power Factor** – A measure of how effectively electrical power is being converted into useful work.

R

- **Renewable Energy Certificates (RECs)** – Market-based instruments that certify electricity was generated from renewable sources.
- **Renewable Portfolio Standard (RPS)** – A policy requiring utilities to source a certain percentage of electricity from renewable sources.

S

- **Smart Grid** – An electricity network that uses digital technology to optimize power distribution and demand response.
- **Spinning Reserve** – Extra generating capacity that can be quickly brought online to maintain grid stability.
- **Substation** – A facility that transforms high-voltage electricity into lower voltage for distribution.

T

- **Terawatt (TW)** – A unit of power equal to **1 trillion watts (10^{12} W)**.
- **Terawatt-hour (TWh)** – A unit of energy representing **1 terawatt of power used for one hour**.
- **Transmission Losses** – Energy lost as electricity travels through power lines over long distances.

V

- **Voltage (V)** – The electrical potential difference that drives current through a circuit.
- **Variable Renewable Energy (VRE)** – Renewable energy sources like wind and solar that fluctuate in output.

References

1. U.S. Energy Information Administration. "Imports and Exports of Oil and Petroleum Products." https://www.eia.gov/energyexplained/oil-and-petroleum-products/imports-and-exports.php

2. U.S. Environmental Protection Agency. "Fast Facts on Transportation Greenhouse Gas Emissions." https://www.epa.gov/greenvehicles/fast-facts-transportation-greenhouse-gas-emissions.

3. U.S. Environmental Protection Agency. "Sources of Greenhouse Gas Emissions." https://www.epa.gov/ghgemissions/sources-greenhouse-gas-emissions#sources.

4. Office of the Historian, U.S. Department of State. "Oil Embargo, 1973–1974." *Milestones in the History of U.S. Foreign Relations.* https://history.state.gov/milestones/1969-1976/oil-embargo.

5. U.S. Energy Information Administration. "How Much Petroleum Does the United States Import and Export?" https://www.eia.gov/tools/faqs/faq.php?id=727&t=6.

   Alternative Fuels Data Center. "Maps and Data." U.S. Department of Energy. https://afdc.energy.gov/data.

6. Belfer Center. "Oil, Conflict, and U.S. National Interests." Harvard Kennedy School. https://www.belfercenter.org/publication/oil-conflict-and-us-national-interests

7. National Oceanic and Atmospheric Administration. "Exxon Valdez." *Damage Assessment, Remediation, and Restoration Program.* https://darrp.noaa.gov/oil-spills/exxon-valdez.

   History.com Editors. "Exxon Valdez Oil Spill." *History*. https://www.history.com/articles/exxon-valdez-oil-spill.

8. History.com Editors. "Bear Stearns Collapses, Sold to J.P. Morgan Chase." *History*. https://www.history.com/this-day-in-history/march-16/bear-stearns-sold-to-j-p-morgan-chase.

   Rodini, Laura. "What Happened to Bear Stearns? Who Bought

It?" *TheStreet*. https://www.thestreet.com/personal-finance/bear-stearns.

9. Federal Deposit Insurance Corporation. "County Bank." *FDIC.gov*. https://www.fdic.gov/resources/resolutions/bank-failures/failed-bank-list/county.html.

   California Department of Financial Protection and Innovation. "State Closes County Bank." Press Release, February 6, 2009. https://dfpi.ca.gov/press_release/state-closes-county-bank/.

10. Gantner, Brennan. "Curtailment and Costs: Are We Wasting Too Much Energy?" *Renewable Energy World*. Published November 12, 2024. https://www.renewableenergyworld.com/solar/utility-scale/curtailment-and-costs-are-we-wasting-too-much-energy/.

    Lawrence Livermore National Laboratory. "Flowcharts." https://flowcharts.llnl.gov/.

11. U.S. Energy Information Administration. "How Much Petroleum Does the United States Import and Export?" https://www.eia.gov/tools/faqs/faq.php?id=727&t=6.

    World Population Review. "US Oil Imports by Country 2025." https://worldpopulationreview.com/country-rankings/us-oil-imports-by-country.

12. American Geosciences Institute. "How Much Oil Does the U.S. Export and Import?" https://profession.americangeosciences.org/society/intersections/faq/how-much-oil-does-us-export-and-import/.

13. Toyota. "2025 Mirai." *Toyota.com*. https://www.toyota.com/mirai/.

14. Lawrence Livermore National Laboratory. "Flowcharts." *LLNL.gov*. Accessed July 28, 2025. https://flowcharts.llnl.gov/.

15. Aniti, Lori. "Solar and Wind Power Curtailments Are Increasing in California." *Today in Energy*. U.S. Energy Information Administration, May 28, 2025.https://www.eia.gov/todayinenergy/detail.php?id=65364.

16. Wilson, Adam. "Curtailment, Congestion Costs Rise as Transmission Upgrades Lag Renewable Growth." *S&P Global Market Intelligence*, November 2, 2023. https://www.spglobal.com/market-intelligence/en/news-insights/research/curtailment-congestion-costs-rise-as-transmission-upgrades-lag-renewable-growth.

17. Warady, Debra, Tyler Hodge, and Lindsay Aramayo. "As Texas Wind and Solar Capacity Increase, Energy Curtailments Are Also Likely to Rise." *Today in Energy*. U.S. Energy Information Administration, July 13, 2023. https://www.eia.gov/todayinenergy/detail.php?id=57100.

    Kennedy, Ryan. "Texas Curtailed 9% of Solar Generation in 2022." *PV Magazine USA. July 14, 2023. https://pv-magazine-usa.com/2023/07/14/texas-curtailed-9-of-solar-generation-in-2022/.*

18. Aniti, Lori, and Susanna Smith. "Why Are Midwest Grid Operators Turning Away Wind Power?" *Today in Energy*. U.S. Energy Information Administration, June 26, 2024. Updated July 1, 2024. https://www.eia.gov/todayinenergy/detail.php?id=62406.

19. Petersen, Melody. "California Utilities Produce More Solar Energy Than the State Can Use." *Governing*, December 2, 2024. https://www.governing.com/resilience/california-utilities-produce-more-solar-energy-than-the-state-can-use.

20. County of Monterey. "2025 Moss Landing Vistra Power Plant Fire." *Ready Monterey County*.https://www.readymontereycounty.org/emergency/2025-moss-landing-vistra-power-plant-fire.

21. California Independent System Operator (CAISO). *Flexible Resources Help Renewables: Fast Facts*. https://www.caiso.com/Documents/FlexibleResourcesHelpRenewables_FastFacts.pdf.

22. **U.S. Department of Energy.** "Advanced Clean Energy Storage." *DOE ADVANCED CLEAN ENERGY STORAGE | Department of Energy*

23. American Chemical Society. "Hydrogen." *Molecule of the Week Archive*. https://www.acs.org/molecule-of-the-week/archive/h/

hydrogen.html.

24. **U.S. EIA.** "Use of Hydrogen." *EIA*. https://www.eia.gov/energyexplained/hydrogen/use-of-hydrogen.php

25. Joseph Gallo Farms. "Environmental Responsibility." https://josephfarms.com/environmental-responsibility/

26. Buggy, Nora, and Dino Klotz. "A (Brief) History of Electrolysis." *Twelve*. https://www.twelve.co/post/a-brief-history-of-electrolysis.

27. Ramirez, Kaitlyn, Tessa Weiss, Thomas Kirk, and Chathurika Gamage. "Hydrogen Reality Check: Distilling Green Hydrogen's Water Consumption." *RMI*, August 2, 2023. https://rmi.org/hydrogen-reality-check-distilling-green-hydrogens-water-consumption/.

28. Tanigawa, Sara. *Fact Sheet: Biogas—Converting Waste to Energy*. Environmental and Energy Study Institute (EESI), October 3, 2017. https://www.eesi.org/papers/view/fact-sheet-biogasconverting-waste-to-energy.

    Pacific Northwest National Laboratory. "Fuel From Sewage Is the Future – and It's Closer Than You Think." *Newswise*, November 2, 2016. https://www.newswise.com/doescience/fuel-from-sewage-is-the-future-and-it-s-closer-than-you-think.

29. U.S. Department of Energy. *Safe Use of Hydrogen*. Office of Energy Efficiency & Renewable Energy. https://www.energy.gov/eere/fuelcells/safe-use-hydrogen.

30. Caltech. "History's Mysteries: Caltech Professor Helps Solve Hindenburg Disaster." *Caltech News*, May 17, 2021. https://www.caltech.edu/about/news/historys-mysteries-caltech-professor-helps-solve-hindenburg-disaster

    Buggy, Nora, and Dino Klotz. "The Hindenburg Disaster: Was Hydrogen Really to Blame?" *H2GP*, July 9, 2025. https://www.h2gp.org/blog-pages/blog/the-hindenburg-disaster-was-hydrogen-really-to-blame.

31. California Independent System Operator (CAISO). *Daily Wind and Solar Real-Time Dispatch and Curtailment Reports.* https://www.caiso.com/library/daily-wind-solar-real-time-dispatch-curtailment-reports

32. Basma, Hussein, and Felipe Rodríguez. *Fuel Cell Electric Tractor-Trailers: Technology Overview and Fuel Economy.* International Council on Clean Transportation, July 18, 2022. https://theicct.org/publication/fuel-cell-tractor-trailer-tech-fuel-jul22/.

33. Pocard, Nicolas. "Ballard Power: Fuel Cell Price to Drop 70–80% as Production Volume Scales." *FuelCellsWorks*, February 12, 2022. https://fuelcellsworks.com/news/ballard-power-fuel-cell-price-to-drop-70-80-as-production-volume-scales.

34. U.S. Energy Information Administration. "How Much Petroleum Does the United States Import and Export?" *Frequently Asked Questions*, last updated March 29, 2024. https://www.eia.gov/tools/faqs/faq.php?id=727&t=6.

35. Grand View Research. *U.S. Energy Transition Market Size, Share & Trends Analysis Report By Type (Renewable Energy, Electrification, Energy Efficiency), By Sector (Power & Utility, Transportation), By Region, And Segment Forecasts, 2025–2033.* https://www.grandviewresearch.com/industry-analysis/us-energy-transition-market-report.

36. UN Atlas of the Oceans. *Tankers and Passenger Ships.* https://www.oceansatlas.org/subtopic/en/c/298/.

37. U.S. Environmental Protection Agency. *Transportation Sector Emissions.* https://www.epa.gov/ghgemissions/transportation-sector-emissions.

38. Martineau, Rebecca. "Fast Flow Future for Heavy-Duty Hydrogen Trucks." *National Renewable Energy Laboratory (NREL)*, June 8, 2022. https://www.nrel.gov/news/detail/program/2022/fast-flow-future-heavy-duty-hydrogen-trucks.

39. U.S. Department of Energy. *How Do Fuel Cell Electric Vehicles*

Work Using Hydrogen? Alternative Fuels Data Center. https://afdc.energy.gov/vehicles/how-do-fuel-cell-electric-cars-work.

40. Lokal_Profil. *Map of North America, Blackout 2003*. Wikimedia Commons. SVG file created August 12, 2007. https://en.wikipedia.org/wiki/File:Map_of_North_America,_blackout_2003.svg.

41. Aguilar, Samantha. "Why Did Austin Lose Power for So Long After an Ice Storm? What to Know." *The Texas Tribune*, February 7, 2023. https://www.texastribune.org/2023/02/07/austin-ice-storm-power-outages-2023/.

42. Shahan, Zachary. "This Chart Shows How California Is Massively Extending Solar Use Into the Evening." *CleanTechnica*, September 24, 2024. https://cleantechnica.com/2024/09/24/this-chart-shows-how-california-is-massively-extending-solar-use-into-the-evening/.

43. Ribeiro, Anna. "Critical Infrastructure Faces 30 Percent Surge in Cyber Attacks, KnowBe4 Report Highlights."*Industrial Cyber*, https://industrialcyber.co/critical-infrastructure/critical-infrastructure-faces-30-percent-surge-in-cyber-attacks-knowbe4-report-highlights/.

44. Aniti, Lori, and Susanna Smith. "Why Are Midwest Grid Operators Turning Away Wind Power?" *U.S. Energy Information Administration*, June 26, 2024. https://www.eia.gov/todayinenergy/detail.php?id=62406.

45. FASTECH. "Can Hydrogen Play a Role in Grid Stabilization?" *FASTECH Blog*, November 26, 2024. https://www.fastechus.com/blog/hydrogen-grid-stabilization.

46. Lewis, Jonathan. "Rural Hospital Invests in Hydrogen." *HFM Magazine*, March 31, 2025. https://www.hfmmagazine.com/rural-hospital-invests-hydrogen.

47. Henry Bergmann, "The History of Water Electrolysis from Its Beginnings to the Present," in *Electrochemical Water Splitting*, ed. J. Scholz and M. Wark (Elsevier, 2022), 231–261, https://www.sciencedirect.com/science/article/abs/pii/B9780128194249000100.

48. Blue Source, LLC. *Life Cycle Analysis Report for Joseph Gallo Farms Biogas to EV Tier 2 LCFS Application*. California Air Resources Board, May 13, 2020. https://ww2.arb.ca.gov/sites/default/files/classic/fuels/lcfs/fuelpathways/comments/tier2/b0089_report.pdf.

49. "Joseph Gallo Farms Moves Closer to Becoming Net-Zero Energy Dairy Farm." *Hoard's Dairyman*, October 7, 2016. https://hoards.com/article-19653-joseph-gallo-farms-moves-closer-to-becoming-net-zero-energy-dairy-farm.html.

Made in the USA
Coppell, TX
19 January 2026

67037670R00060